S0-AJP-368

Presenting Performances
A Handbook for Sponsors

Thomas Wolf
Illustrated by Barbara Carter

Fifth Edition 1983

This book was originally published by
The New England Foundation for the Arts.

AMERICAN COUNCIL FOR THE ARTS
570 Seventh Avenue, New York, NY 10018

Additional copies may be obtained from:

American Council for the Arts
570 Seventh Avenue
New York, NY 10018
(212) 354-6655

ISBN: 0-915400-45-6

Funds for the original publication of this book were provided by:

Connecticut Commission on the Arts
Maine State Commission on the Arts and Humanities
Massachusetts Council on the Arts and Humanities
New Hampshire Commission on the Arts
Rhode Island State Council on the Arts
Vermont Council on the Arts
National Endowment for the Arts

Design: The Laughing Bear Associates, Montpelier, Vermont

Copyright New England Foundation for the Arts, Inc. 1977.
No part of this book may be reproduced in any form without written permission.

Preface

Since it first came off the press in February of 1977, this book has proven to be one of the best sellers in the field of arts administration. The first edition sold out in two months. Orders came in, not for single copies, but for 25, 50, even 100 copies at a time. A second and a third edition followed and, by the end of 1981, 14,000 copies were in print.

Why has the book been so popular? Partly we think, because it is well written and has engaging illustrations. But over and above its readability is the obvious market for this kind of guide. In the last fifteen years there has been a dramatic increase in the number of organizations which sponsor performances. Spurred on by the encouragement of federal and state funding, these organizations have brought about a renaissance in live performances to millions of Americans.

It was partly because we saw this trend in our New England region that the Board of the New England Foundation for the Arts encouraged Tom Wolf to write *Presenting Performances*. For over a decade, we had seen the development of small community-based sponsoring organizations. Increasingly, it was these organizations which were making performing arts events available to New England people, serving as a crucial delivery system in the region. As the importance of these organizations became apparent, our agencies created special funding arrangements to support them. But we were also keenly aware that creating programs and giving money was not the only way we could be helpful. Over the years, many sponsors had come to us and said, "If only there were a book that provided good, solid practical information. That is something we really need." We realized that a book like *Presenting Performances* would have an eager audience and a ready market.

It had always been our hope that someday this book would find its place among the American Council for the Arts' fine family of publications. As *the* recognized publisher of books on arts administration, the American Council for the Arts could introduce *Presenting Performances* to a whole new group of readers. Perhaps we were also convinced that *Persenting Performances,* born of the wisdom and wit of our New England region, had at last come of age and it was time to share it even more widely.

So here, once again, is Thomas Wolf's *Presenting Performances* in its fifth edition. Barbara Carter has again captured the joys and frustrations of performing arts sponsorship in her much acclaimed line drawings. All of the old material is in this new edition as well. You can still learn the secrets of fund raising, the romance of Board selection, and the fine art of selling tickets and designing promotional materials. Revealed to you are the mysteries of performers' eating habits as well as deserved moments of moodiness. The book is full of practical information, but, judging by the reaction to earlier editions, we trust you will find it entertaining as well.

A book like this is never finished. It needs updating and revisions as new fashions of presentations emerge and new management methods are discovered. So let's treat Tom Wolf's book as community property and have everyone take part in helping him prepare the next edition. If you have differences of opinion with the approaches or examples, please tell him. If you have found a new way of dealing with an old problem please share it. Tom is a musician; he has a good ear and is a professional listener — which is one reason why this is such a good book.

We hope you enjoy it.

Robb Hankins, Executive Director
New Hampshire Commission on the Arts

Anne Hawley, Executive Director
Massachusetts Council on the Arts and Humanities

Ellen McCulloch-Lovell, Executive Director
Vermont Council on the Arts

Christina White, Executive Director
Rhode Island State Council on the Arts

Alden Wilson, Executive Director
Maine State Commission on the Arts and Humanities

Gary Young, Executive Director
Connecticut Commission on the Arts

Introduction

There are many organizations that present performances. But of them, only a small percentage have large budgets and few are staffed by professional arts administrators. Most sponsoring organizations are small, community-based enterprises staffed largely by volunteers. The number of performances which these organizations sponsor every year is staggering. There is no official count, but the number, in New England alone, must be in the tens of thousands. The arts marketplace depends on these organizations and this book has been written primarily for the people who run them.

Presenting Performances has been called a handbook for sponsors and, for some, that word may need clarification. A sponsor is a person who is connected with an organization which presents performances — connected either as a paid worker, a board member, or a volunteer. Another term for a sponsor is a presenter. In contrast to an arts administrator who is always a paid professional, a sponsor (or presenter) can be someone who contributes a few hours of time. There has long been a need for a book which provides this person with basic information about performing arts sponsorship. For paid staff and Board members as well, few books provide the kind of practical advice that is so often necessary.

Several years ago, the Western States Arts Foundation published a pamphlet for sponsors presenting dance touring audiences. The publication, brief as it was, contained much reliable information and was an immediate success. This book is an extension of that initial effort. Its intended audience is broader, and it provides more detail. Yet it is organized around the same basic issues, and its purpose is the same: to help sponsors do a better job.

A book of this kind is generally the work of numerous contributors. Many people read this manuscript in draft and made suggestions. They include: Jane Doerfer, Greg Fisher, Joel Goldberg, Fred Goldstein, Dan Savage, Neil Sullivan, Sue Taylor, Craig Watson, and my parents, Irene and Walter Wolf. The advice of all of these people greatly improved the final version.

Two men especially deserve credit for much of the wisdom in these pages — Boris Goldovsky and Andrew Wolf. Working closely with both of these enormously experienced performer / administrators over the last fifteen years, I have picked up innumerable tricks of the trade. Many of their secrets have been passed on in these pages in the form of anecdotal information.

To consultant, Mary Van Someren Cok; to editors, Fred Goldstein and Jennifer Shotwell; to designers Mason Singer and Linda Mirabile; and to illustrator, Barbara Carter — special thanks is due. All of these people contributed toward making this book more readable and more attractive. I would also like to thank Robert Porter and the staff of the American Council for the Arts for their help in undertaking this new edition of *Presenting Performances*.

Finally, my thanks to the executive directors of the six New England state arts agencies who wrote the Preface to *Presenting Performances*. This project was their idea from the start, and it was in large measure due to their encouragement that the project came to fruition.

Thomas Wolf
Fall, 1983

Contents

Preface
by the six New England state arts agency executive directors

Introduction

Contents

Chapter 1 — Administration

Rule 1 — Get ORGANIZED! 14
Rule 2 — Incorporate and file for TAX-EXEMPT STATUS. 14
Rule 3 — Pick your Trustees with UTMOST CARE. 19
Rule 4 — Give your Board of Trustees a WORKING STRUCTURE 22
Rule 5 — MAXIMIZE your work force. 23
Rule 6 — Spend your dollars where they COUNT. 26
Rule 7 — KNOW the LAW. 29
Rule 8 — When it comes to money, BE CAUTIOUS. 32

Chapter 2 — Performers

Rule 9 — Remember, performers are PEOPLE too. 39
Rule 10 — DON'T buy a pig in a poke. 40
Rule 11 — It's often NEGOTIABLE. 43
Rule 12 — INSIST on a contract. 46
Rule 13 — Utilize your performers FULLY. 51
Rule 14 — PREPARE your performers. 54
Rule 15 — Be a good PARENT to your performers. 57

Chapter 3 — Filling the Auditorium

Rule 16 — You have to MAKE it happen. 61
Rule 17 — Check the COMPETITION. 62
Rule 18 — Start your subscription campaign EARLY. 64
Rule 19 — Write EXCITING promotional copy. 65
Rule 20 — Work CLOSELY with newspapers. 68
Rule 21 — Use the RADIO and TV too. 72
Rule 22 — Use publicity materials that look PROFESSIONAL. ... 74
Rule 23 — In ticket pricing, DEMAND fair market value. 78
Rule 24 — Make the night of the performance
             something SPECIAL. 82

Chapter 4 — Fund Raising

Rule 25 — Don't FANTASIZE. 87
Rule 26 — Keep your OBJECTIVES in sight. 88
Rule 27 — Make it EASY to contribute to your organization. 91
Rule 28 — Remember your local BUSINESSES. 92
Rule 29 — Concentrate your efforts on
             INDIVIDUAL contributors. 96
Rule 30 — If you must chase a rainbow,
             READ THIS SECTION. 101
Rule 31 — When dealing with public funding
             agencies, PERSEVERE. 104

Chapter 5 — Behind the Curtain

Rule 32 — Don't buy a RUBE GOLDBERG! 112
Rule 33 — Know your SPACE. 113
Rule 34 — For outdoor performances, avoid a
             DESERT ISLAND or TIMES SQUARE. 116
Rule 35 — Remember, on every outdoor festival, a little
             RAIN must fall. 119
Rule 36 — Know the UNION rules. 122
Rule 37 — Hire RELIABLE technical help. 125
Rule 38 — Supply proper equipment that WORKS. 129
Rule 39 — Be PREPARED. 131

Appendices

Appendix A — Sample Bylaws...................... 138
Appendix B — Sample Contracts.................... 143
Appendix C — Sample Press Release 150
Appendix D — Sample Fund-Raising Letter 151
Appendix E — Procedure for Applying to the
                 National Endowment for the Arts 152
Appendix F — Technical Glossary..................... 155

Get ORGANIZED!

Chapter 1
Administration

Once upon a time there was a young man who decided that he would devote his life to the arts. The only question was, Which one? He set out for the local music conservatory and presented himself to a piano teacher. "To play piano," he was told, "you will have to practice scales two hours a day for the rest of your life." Surprised and a bit disappointed, the young man walked across the street to the art institute and told his story to the instructor of painting. "To become a painter," he was told, "you will have to learn first to draw simple shapes; later, we will let you paint still lifes of fruit and flowers." The local academy of drama was next. Our hero wanted *Hamlet*; the teacher suggested six months of calisthenics. Finally, in desperation, the young man paid a call on the local concert agency. No sooner had he walked into the office and presented his case than he was seated at a typewriter and told to produce a press release for the next day's event. ("Suddenly, I was learning how to write excellent fiction," he later recalled.) As soon as he finished the press release, he was dispatched to the florist and told to arrange a display of flowers for the auditorium stage, ("What better way to show off my artistic eye!") Finally, when he returned to the office, he was given a list of phone numbers and told to sell tickets for the next day's event. ("Instantly I learned the rudiments of persuasive play acting.") By the end of the day, the young man had made up his mind. The most creative life in the arts was not in music, painting, or theatre; it was in the promotion and sponsorship of performing arts events.

The story is, of course, apocryphal, but it is included here to introduce the idea that performing arts sponsorship can be an extremely satisfying and creative occupation whether you are a volunteer worker, a

Board member, or a paid administrator. Lest the story mislead, however, we must quickly point out that, contrary to the young man's notions, creative sponsors are probably not the ones who simply arrange flowers and sell tickets. Rather they are the ones who can engage in long-range planning, can set realistic goals, and can achieve these goals through efficient management.

Rule 1 — Get ORGANIZED!

One sponsor puts it this way: "Everything must begin with sensible planning. In our case, it did not. By just letting things happen we learned our lessons the hard way. For example, we learned that it is essential to think about fund raising *before* you need money. Today, we find ourselves back on track. We think one or two seasons ahead. We project budgets; we set artistic and administrative goals. For me personally, the most exciting part is getting organized and translating those goals into reality."

In the course of this chapter, we will consider some of the critical issues in arts administration. It will become clear that arts organizations need far more than gifted performers. They need people with business acumen, some knowledge of law, and a talent for efficiency and good organization. We will also see that the skillful sponsor is one who has developed what I have elsewhere called "the mentality of creative parsimony"* — the notion that, for any particular endeavor, there is always a less expensive way.

Rule 2 — Incorporate and file for TAX-EXEMPT STATUS.

If your organization is not tax-exempt, a potential contributor will not give you the time of day.

"Why a corporation?" many new sponsors ask, "We are simply a handful of people — all volunteers — handling a tiny budget. Isn't the idea of forming a corporation a bit out of scale with the scope of our activities?" The answer to this question is probably "no." A corporate structure allows your organization to apply for tax-exempt status, to enter into contracts with performers, to limit personal liability, and to secure credit. Without a corporate structure, carrying out the daily chores of the office soon becomes complicated: potential contributors turn their backs on you, stores refuse to open charge accounts, and indi-

---

*Cf. Boris Goldovsky and Thomas Wolf, *Touring Opera*, National Opera Association, 1975.

Incorporate
and file
for TAX-
EXEMPT
STATUS.

viduals must be found who will take personal responsibility for signing contracts.

By far the most important advantage of a corporate structure is that it allows your organization to apply for and secure tax-exempt status — a process which generally takes about six months. Once tax-exempt status has been granted, individuals or businesses can contribute to the organization and deduct the donations for income-tax purposes. As a general rule, almost no one contributes to organizations that are not tax-exempt — it is simply too expensive to do so. Therefore, unless you can do without fund raising, you must either incorporate or become associated with an organization which is itself tax-exempt.

The arrangement by which a small sponsoring organization becomes a "project" of a larger tax-exempt institution is a common solution to the problem of incorporation for those who do not want to go to the time, expense, and trouble of incorporating themselves. According to this arrangement, the arts group might associate itself with the local church, college, or YMCA. In doing so, however, the arts organization loses its autonomy and is subject to the whims of the parent organization's Board of Trustees. Sometimes the arrangement lasts indefinitely, but often trouble begins to brew when the growing arts organization begins to expand its programming. A nervous Board of Trustees starts to feel uneasy about a large budget which is not under its close scrutiny. Many groups which begin as a project of a larger organization eventually find that separate incorporation is desirable.

However, this "umbrella" arrangement is an excellent temporary solution to the problem of securing tax-exempt contributions for new enterprises. Let us say that a group of people wants to set up a sponsoring organization, and each agrees to contribute $200 to the new venture. Since the organization is not tax-exempt, the contributions are not tax-deductible. However, if, during the first few months, the new organization can be listed as a project of the YMCA (or some other tax-exempt entity), then a separate account can be set up and checks can be drawn to "YMCA — ARTS ACCOUNT." In this way, contributions can be solicited from the first day of the new project with the understanding that they are tax-deductible.

For an individual without legal training, the procedures connected with incorporation and securing tax-exempt status are complicated and mysterious. For lawyers, however, these same procedures are fairly routine; moreover, it is not uncommon for lawyers to donate their services in incorporating a nonprofit organization. Often a lawyer will be invited to serve on the Board of Trustees after the corporation is formed. If a public-spirited lawyer cannot be found in your community, call your state arts council. This agency may run a referral service on free or low-cost legal assistance for arts-related activities. Another possibility is to call your county or state bar association and to ask for a referral in your area.

Your lawyer will be busy during the first year of your new corporation. (After the first year, you will probably not need legal assistance very often.) The first thing that the lawyer will do is write up your Articles of Organization and file these, together with the necessary forms, at the appropriate state offices. The cost of filing is modest — usually well under $50. Once your organization has been granted corporate status, the incorporators must draw up a set of by-laws which follow a standard format for nonprofit corporations (cf. Appendix A). As your lawyer will no doubt tell you, the Internal Revenue Service (IRS) will review your bylaws carefully in determining whether or not you qualify as a tax-exempt corporation.

The bylaws should be flexible and the Board should feel free to amend them whenever necessary. As one lawyer puts it, "In the bylaws, almost nothing is forever." From the very beginning, however, try to set things up so that corporate decisions can be made quickly and easily. Moreover, your lawyer may suggest a number of items that you feel are unnecessary, but unless they appear to run counter to your plans, let them remain in the document. There is a formula for writing bylaws and the IRS does not like to see certain familiar paragraphs deleted.

After the bylaws are written, your lawyer will file an application for tax-exempt status. If everything goes smoothly, you can expect to receive a federal tax-exemption letter within several months. If there are any problems with your application, the IRS will send a letter to your organization suggesting certain revisions in the bylaws or the Articles of Organization.

Once you have received tax-exempt status, the difficult part is over. However, it is a mistake to cease thinking about the corporate obligations of the Board of Trustees. The Trustees must meet at certain times; minutes must be kept when meetings are held; and financial records must be filed with various state and federal agencies. All the records of the corporation (Articles of Organization, bylaws, tax-exemption letter, minutes, financial statements, etc.) should be kept together since they are open to scrutiny by state and federal authorities at any time. A common procedure is to put all records in a three-hole, loose-leaf binder which can be left with the Clerk of the corporation, with your attorney, or at the organization's office.

It is important to remember that potential contributors, government agencies, and business concerns tend to take a different attitude toward a legally-constituted nonprofit corporation than toward even the most respected and distinguished group of people which is loosely banded together. Armed with a Federal Employers Identification number (which is like a social security number for corporations) and a tax-exemption letter, your legal and organizational status will be clear to everyone, and your dealings with the outside world will be appreciably less complicated.

Pick your Trustees with UTMOST CARE.

Rule 3 —
Pick your Trustees with
UTMOST CARE.

Use at least as much discretion in choosing Trustees as in selecting
performing groups. Disinterested people make poor Trustees.*

Recently the executive director of a state arts council said the following in a speech to arts administrators: ''It seems remarkable to me that
many of our arts organizations which maintain such high aesthetic stan-
dards are incredibly casual about their choice of Trustees. 'How is it,' I
often ask myself, 'that an organization which subjects all of its performers to the most rigorous scrutiny can be so unconcerned about the selection of people who will, after all, have ultimate responsibility for running the corporation? Bad performers can be fired. But try to get rid of a
bad Board member and you will see how difficult it is.' '' The speaker
then went on to give sound advice on the selection of good Trustees.

First, think of every member of the Board of Trustees as someone
with a specific job or responsibility. Do not invite anyone to serve simply because you think his or her name is important to your organization's credibility. Window dressing (i.e., the use of distinguished names
as an endorsement) can be achieved by forming a special committee of
honorary advisors. Mayors, senators, famous performers, wealthy individuals, and others can be asked to lend their names to your endeavor
by serving on an ''Advisory Committee'' which may never meet and is
essentially powerless. This will allow you to put their names on your let-
terhead without inviting them to serve on the Board of Trustees.

Second, every Trustee should have a fixed term of office which should
not exceed three years. If, at the end of the term, the Board member has
performed well, he or she can be reelected to another term. But reap-
pointment should not be automatic, and members of the corporation
who vote on such matters should evaluate the Trustee's performance
carefully before reelecting.

Third, in searching out Board members, begin by deciding what jobs
and responsibilities need to be covered. Does the Board need someone
with expertise in law or business? Could a Certified Public Accountant
be found who would be willing to assist in setting up the books? Is a
major contributor needed who can be counted on for at least $500 each
year? Perhaps the Trustees feel that they need to seek a minority member in order to represent more of the community. Or perhaps there is a
particular job, such as head of the promotion committee, that needs to
be filled. Any of these are good reasons to appoint specific people with
proper qualifications to the Board. Match the organization's needs to

---

*In many corporations, Trustees are referred to as ''Directors.'' For sim-
plicity, this section will always refer to them as ''Trustees'' and will refer
to Boards of Directors as ''Boards of Trustees.''

particular people with particular skills. Do not begin by saying, "Mrs. J. would be so pleased to be on the Board; she simply loves the concerts." Instead, think of the jobs that need to be done and find the best people to do them.

Fourth, do not hedge when you invite someone to serve on the Board. Tell the person why he or she is being asked. Be very direct about the responsibilities that are to be assumed. If a business executive is being put on the Board in order to attract more funds from the business community, this fact should be clearly stated: "The Board would like to increase business contributions by $2,000 over the next three years, and we would like you to be responsible for organizing the effort." If prospective Board members turn you down, consider yourself lucky. You have been spared the frustration of putting up with people who would not be doing their share of the work.

One of the most persistent problems facing small sponsoring organizations is that their Boards of Trustees do not take proper initiative in fund raising. In many cases, Board members do not even realize that if they approve a deficit budget, they must help devise a sensible plan for raising the necessary funds. Many believe that the responsibility for raising funds rests with the staff. Some Trustees give ten or twenty dollars each year and believe that their obligations in this area have been met.

In fact, of course, nearly every organization that has vigorous fund-raising activities should have a Board of Trustees that is very much involved in those activities. On some Boards, each Trustee is made personally responsible for a certain sum of money — sometimes as much as $1,000 or more. The Trustees can either contribute the money themselves or raise it from among friends and acquaintances. On other Boards, the Trustees take an active role in the collective fund-raising effort, with at least one task or obligation assigned to each Trustee. Regardless of the particular plan the Board ultimately adopts, it is essential that each new Trustee is made aware of specific obligations in this area. As one sponsor puts it: "If our Board were not involved in fund-raising, we would be out of business in a year. At least 30% of our contributions come from Board members, and at least 60% of our donations are Board solicited. In addition, for big projects or in the case of unexpected financial reversals, we ask the Board for special help. If the staff does not have this kind of support from its Trustees, it becomes severely handicapped in its activities."

Finally, it is essential to keep in mind that the Board of Trustees is the ultimate authority, legally speaking, on all decisions affecting the corporation which it serves. In most cases, the Trustees' authority is delegated to the staff, which then carries out the daily operation of the organization. Nevertheless, according to the corporation's bylaws, such delegation of authority can be rescinded by the Board at any time. Thus, the Trustees' power is, at least theoretically, virtually absolute; and any staff member who does not take an active interest in the Board's activities and composition is risking a great deal, both personally and in relation to the future activities of the organization.

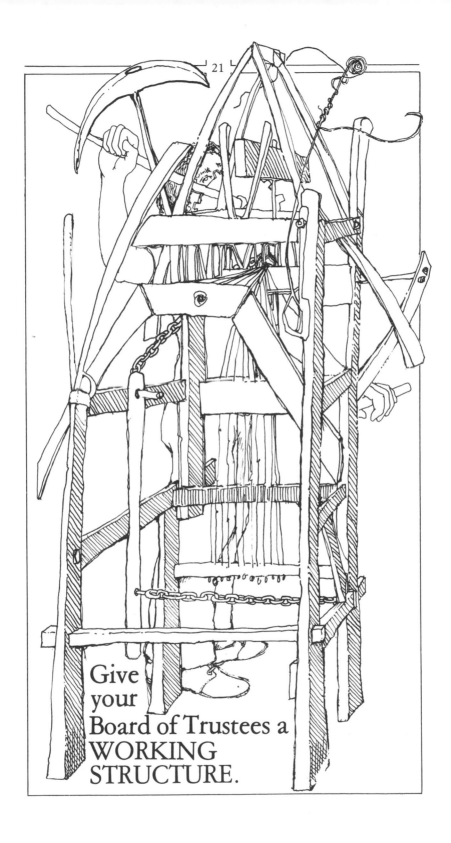

Give
your
Board of Trustees a
WORKING
STRUCTURE.

Rule 4 —
Give your Board a
WORKING STRUCTURE.

In addition to strong officers, you need a well-defined committee structure to carry out the important work of the corporation.

The full Board of Trustees meets at least once a year at the corporation's annual meeting. But the real work of the Board will not be carried out when so many people gather together for prolonged discussion on long-range issues and immediate business. Rather, most of the work will be carried out when small subdivisions of the Board form committees to carry out specific tasks assigned to them. Usually, every member of the Board will be asked to serve on at least one committee.*

The committee structure has become the butt of many jokes because, all too often, it becomes so complex and overextended that one committee undermines the work of another. Communication breaks down, and the coherence of the work effort is reduced. However, effective committee organization can usually be maintained when there is strong administrative direction from above. This is one reason why the office of President of the Board of Trustees is such a critical position. Given a strong, well-organized President, one who supervises and requires periodic reporting from the committees, the corporation can usually maintain excellent cohesion and internal organization. Do not, therefore, elect a Board President on any but the most pragmatic grounds. Find the strongest candidate for the job. If you feel you must recognize a particular person's contribution to the organization — but the person is clearly unqualified administratively for the President's job — you have the alternative of appointing an Honorary President.

Like the President, the Treasurer and the Clerk (or Secretary) of the corporation must be chosen carefully with specific qualifications in mind. The Treasurer will be responsible for making the financial reports to the Board (and in certain instances, to state and federal agencies). In some organizations, the Treasurer may be expected to sign checks, arrange for audits, approve small changes in the budget, and keep tabs on the staff's use of money. Obviously, someone with financial expertise is needed in this job. The Clerk (or Secretary) of the corporation must keep accurate records of meetings, circulate minutes, send out official notification of upcoming meetings, and certify specific resolutions of the Board. A well-organized person is needed for this job — one who can type or who has access to a good secretary.

Among the committees, the one charged with the greatest adminis-

---

*Committees need not be made up exclusively of Board members. In fact, it is theoretically possible to have committees on which no Board members serve. As long as a committee's activity and membership is approved by the Board, anyone may serve.

trative responsibility is the Executive Committee. Members of this committee include the Officers of the corporation and other Trustees concerned with the organization's business and fiscal affairs. It is important to keep this committee small enough so that decisions can be made quickly and easily. In fact, one of its major purposes is to avoid the necessity of convening the entire Board every time a Trustee decision is called for. The full Board delegates its authority to the Executive Committee, which then becomes an extremely powerful decision-making body. Because of this, members of this committee must go out of their way to make other Board members feel useful and needed. The best way to accomplish this is to give each Board member a responsible job on another committee.

Most other committees are organized for specific purposes: ticket selling, promotion, entertainment, business and corporate support, building, long-range planning, flowers and other amenities, housing, and so forth. Sometimes only two or three people are needed to take responsibility for a certain area (e.g., ''Hospitality''); at other times, a large group may be required as is usually the case on the Fund-raising Committee.

At a recent conference, an arts administrator commented on the need for a committee structure: "When I took over my organization fifteen years ago, I had to run around opening the building for rehearsals, making sure fresh flowers were on the stage before performances, picking up programs from the printers, distributing posters, approaching local businesses for donations, and preparing the direct mailings. I was overextended! Today things are different; I do not do any of the tasks. They are all done by committee members.'' This particular administrator, incidentally, runs one of the most successful concert series in New England.

Rule 5 —
MAXIMIZE your work force.

Full-time employees are a luxury that most small sponsoring organizations cannot afford. Use volunteers, hire part-time people, and contract out as much work as you can.

When it comes to hiring staff, arts organizations find themselves in a dilemma. Money, particularly money for administration, is always in short supply, and qualified employees are expensive. The best candidates for arts administration posts are people with a strong background both in the arts and in business; but if these candidates are very good, they are usually able to market themselves effectively into well-paying jobs — ones which not only pay adequate salaries, but pay medical and retirement benefits as well. Thus, in 1977, it is not unreasonable to expect to pay anywhere from $12,000 to $20,000 in salary and benefits to a qualified arts administrator. For the great majority of sponsoring organizations, this figure is too high; for some, it exceeds the total

MAXIMIZE
your work force.

amount appropriated for all administrative costs. Clearly, alternatives must be found.

Some community-based sponsoring organizations are staffed entirely by volunteers. Most of the larger ones pay at least one person for administrative work. But in the majority of cases, full-time paid administrators are unnecessary. Some of the most successful organizations have a staff of one, two, or three people (including a director) all of whom are part-time. Since the demand for interesting part-time work has increased steadily in recent years, it is not unusual to find remarkably competent people to fill these kinds of jobs.

Sponsoring organizations soon realize the advantage of a part-time staff. Part-time employees can be quite productive, often working more hours than they have been hired for; usually, they are not paid benefits, while full-time staff often expect benefits; and, if they are hired as "independent contractors," the sponsoring organization need not withhold taxes from their paychecks. Finally, salary scales figured on a per-hour basis tend to be lower for part-time employees (e.g., two half-timers will collectively receive less salary than one full-timer).

As it is for administrators, so it is for clerical help. A full-time secretary may earn $9,000/year plus another $1,000 for benefits. But few sponsoring organizations really need or can afford this luxury. Part-time clerical workers can be hired for as little as $3.00 per hour with no additional costs incurred for benefits of any kind. Most organizations expect a secretary to act as a combination receptionist/phone-answerer/typist; but for an organization which is interested in saving money, only the last task may require the assistance of an additional paid person. Sponsoring organizations do not generally need a receptionist, and if, in certain cases, it is thought desirable to have one, the position can be filled by a volunteer. Answering the phone is generally not a problem when people are in the office; when everyone is out, the phone can be answered by a machine (purchase price: $150-$200) or by an answering service. As far as typing is concerned, part-time clerical help is easy to find.

Contracting out work (i.e., hiring people to do specific tasks and paying them by the hour or the job) is an extremely efficient and inexpensive way to get work done. Independent contractors are very productive; they do not get paid to sit around the office, chat, and wait for work to come in. Generally, they are especially well qualified to do the work you have hired them for; they are specialists while someone on a full-time staff may not be equipped with the same special skills. In addition, if you are not pleased with the work of an independent contractor, you need not go through the mental anguish of deciding whether or not to fire the person. If the job is poorly done, you simply do not rehire the person the next time a similar job must be done.

Ten years ago, a great deal of arts administration work was done by unpaid volunteers. In the decade since then, there has been a decline in volunteer work due in part to the professionalization of arts administrators and the changing attitudes toward careers among younger women.

Nonetheless, a good deal of work for sponsoring organizations is still done by volunteers, both male and female. Often a professional staff works closely with volunteers on such tasks as selling tickets, distributing promotion, designing publicity materials, meeting and entertaining performers, evaluating residencies, training ushers, arranging fund-raising events, and so forth. Most organizations could not make do without the services of volunteers, and it is important to cultivate a large group of hard-working people who believe enough in your activities to lend a helping hand. However, remember that "A volunteer is an employee who cannot be fired" and choose your volunteers carefully matching the proper person with the right job.

Rule 6 — Spend your dollars where they COUNT.

Use your ingenuity to save money on administrative expenses. Work at home, mail in bulk, and get other organizations to sell your tickets.

There is nothing that gives a young arts administrator more of a thrill than taking over an office. Perhaps this explains why so many of them occupy expensive office space when a rent-free office at home would suffice. Some of the most successful administrators work out of their basements or in converted bedrooms. By choosing to work at home, administrators do a service both to their organizations and to themselves: the organizations save money on rent and the administrators are eligible for a tax deduction on the home offices. It is true that, for some, there are too many distractions at home, and an office away from home is a necessity. In that case, the organization should make a concerted effort to find donated office space. This is usually not difficult to find since contributed office space allows the donor a tax deduction.

There are a number of service options when the organization considers investing in a telephone. In order to list your organization's phone number, you must pay at business rates, which often run as much as twice that of individual monthly service. Some organizations are willing to pay the extra charge in order to allow potential ticket buyers to find their number in the phone book. Others encourage the director to keep the phone listed in his or her own name and then proceed to list this home number in all promotional materials. The prospective ticket buyer who sees the publicity will know where to call, and the organization does not have to pay the more expensive business rates.

The whole issue is simplified considerably when pre-performance phone orders are taken at a different location — a local bookstore, record store, or gift shop. Many of these in-town shops are willing to sell the tickets in exchange for the free publicity they receive. The reasoning goes something like this: people who have the money to buy tickets for a performing arts event make good customers for other things as

Spend your dollars where they COUNT.

well. Thus, if tickets are sold at the local bookstore, prospective book customers can be lured into the store when they come to purchase their tickets. In this manner, most sponsoring organizations can find other business concerns which are willing to handle the pre-performance sale of tickets. Since these concerns do have phone numbers listed in the directory, the sponsoring organization does not have to worry about having its own business listing. It simply makes known in its publicity where tickets can be purchased.

Nonprofit organizations which do a large amount of direct mailing can save significant amounts of money by getting a nonprofit, bulk-rate mailing permit from the post office. In a city, you can call the ''Mailing Requirements'' section at the central post office to request an application; in rural areas, it can be requested from your local post office. The initial application costs $20, and an organization must pay a yearly fee of $40. However, the savings on third-class mailings of over 200 items is considerable. At approximately .02 per piece of mail, you save over $20.00 on a mailing of 200 items. If your mailing has 1,000 letters, you save more than $100. There is a good deal of sorting and bundling involved (you must sort by zip code, which can be very time consuming if the mailing list is not properly arranged), but if you are planning to do several mailings each year, you should look into this alternative.

Finally, in preparing mailing lists, find out whether other organizations in your area have inexpensive services you can purchase or barter for. If you are located in a major city, many arts service organizations can now provide you with mailing labels which contain the names and addresses of would-be ticket buyers. The cost of the labels is modest, and since the organization probably updates the names and addresses regularly, the list itself is quite valuable. (Your state arts council can probably tell you whether such a service is available in your community.) Alternatively, other community service organizations might be very interested in pooling their mailing lists with yours. If your list has been well maintained and is up-to-date,* it is a valuable asset which can be used as barter. If you are not anxious to circulate it or if other organizations do not see it as valuable to their interests, you can still offer to purchase their lists for a modest sum.

There are always many ways to save money in the administrative domain without lowering the quality of what your organization is doing.

---

*The importance of reliable, up-to-date mailing lists should be underscored. One person should be responsible for making necessary changes as people move or as deaths and divorces occur. In addition to a general mailing list, it is useful to maintain a card file of all people who have either purchased tickets or given a contribution. On the card you can indicate the year of the purchase or contribution as well as the amount paid. This is very helpful in planning telephone follow-ups to mailings (e.g., ''We just wanted to make sure you received our fund-raising letter. We so appreciated the $50 you gave last year and would welcome any amount again this year.'')

All of the alternatives should be investigated since, in the long run, they may add up to the only formula for survival.

Rule 7 —
KNOW the LAW.

If you want to avoid ulcers and headaches, become familiar with the laws governing withholding, unemployment compensation, and social security. In addition, keep a calendar with entries indicating when various state and federal forms must be filed.

Every organization must meet certain obligations both to its employees and to the federal and state governments. An organization with salaried employees must withhold taxes from their paychecks and, in some cases, pay social security and unemployment taxes. In the case of corporations, additional returns must be filed periodically. If sponsors know what their obligations are and if they are careful to meet all of them on time, numerous problems can be avoided; in some cases money can also be saved.

Many sponsoring organizations avoid complicated bookkeeping and pay procedures by treating all employees as if they were "independent contractors." Since these employees work flexible hours, are part-time, and/or are hired for specific tasks, it is fairly simple to justify this procedure. The organization pays a *fee* (it is essential not to call it a salary) and neither withholds income taxes nor pays social security taxes. If an independent contractor earns more than $600 in a particular calendar year, the organization is obligated to report these earnings to the IRS on Form 1099. The form can be obtained from the IRS or from a local bank or post office. It should be filled out after January 1st with one copy going to the employee and another to the IRS.

When an organization has employees over whom it dictates specified working hours, days off, vacations, etc., and if these employees are full-time, it is more difficult to justify the "independent contractor" designation and the pay procedure is more complicated. Each salaried employee must fill out a W-4 Form claiming the number of exemptions he or she is entitled to. Each pay period the organization withholds taxes from each salary. The amounts deducted are computed with the aid of tables contained in the IRS' *Circular E* and in publications from the state or local taxing authority. These taxes must be deposited by specific dates, ranging from four times each month to quarterly, depending on the amount of taxes to be remitted. The funds are usually deposited at the organization's commercial bank. It is absolutely essential that the deposits are made on time. When they are late, strict fines are imposed. All too often, an organization has spent the deducted taxes on some other pressing financial commitment and cannot come up with the needed cash before the deadline. If your organization finds itself in this position, it is best to borrow the money and to pay on time.

Just as with independent contractors, the earnings of salaried em-

ployees must be reported after the first of January. A W-2 Form is used for this purpose. This form allows the organization to show how much was paid to the employee and how much was deducted for tax payments. One copy goes to the employer, one to the IRS, and one to the state taxing authority.

The procedure with social security (or FICA) taxes has recently changed and the new laws have had a severe impact on the budgets of many arts organizations. With independent contractors, of course, nonprofit corporations do not have any FICA obligations; but many have not paid FICA to salaried staff either since the federal tax determination letter generally specified that the organizations were exempt from FICA as well as federal unemployment taxes (FUTA). New laws, however, require non-profit organizations to participate in the social security system as of January, 1984. According to the law, both employees and employers must contribute to FICA in equal amounts. The amount in 1984 was 7% of the first $35,700 of each employee's salary. This has taken an additional bite out of the budgets of many organizations and has made the hiring of independent contractors even more attractive.

Some nonprofit corporations manage to offer retirement benefits to all their employees (whether salaried or in the independent contractor class) by making use of Individual Retirement Accounts. This plan involves considerably less bookkeeping for the employer than social security, and the financial return is usually better for the employee. Information on this plan can be provided by almost any bank.

Nonprofit corporations are exempt from paying federal unemployment taxes, but the case with state unemployment taxes (or state unemployment "insurance") is less clear. Many performing groups do pay state unemployment insurance so that their employees (performers with long periods of unemployment) can collect compensation. Other nonprofit corporations (such as sponsoring organizations) may elect not to pay since usually the state offers that option. However, if the number of salaried employees increases beyond three or four, this policy may become risky since organizations not paying state unemployment insurance must pay 100% of their employees' claims if the employees' work for the organization is terminated. Before making a final decision on this matter, it would be wise to consult the organization's accountant.

Nonprofit corporations that have over $25,000 of gross receipts in any year are required to file a Form 990 with the IRS. This form must be filed no later than the 15th day of the fifth month after the annual accounting period ends. Fines for filing late are steep, though extensions can be requested for up to six months providing a Form 2758 is filed before the normal deadline. Since Form 990 is essentially an accounting document, it is wise to consider having it prepared by a Certified Public Accountant (CPA). Services by CPA's need not be expensive if you do not ask the accountant to audit the organization's accounting records. Unaudited financial statements will usually satisfy the small organization's needs though some states do require audited statements from any organizations with gross revenues in excess of a specified amount. The accountant's fee will usually depend on the scope of what he is being asked to do and all organizations should clarify in advance both the basis for computing the CPA's fee as well as the extent of the services to be provided. Much of the cost of an accountant's services can be avoided if the organization has had the foresight to place a CPA on the Board. However, remember, if an audit is required, it must be done by an *independent* CPA, not one connected with the organization and serving on its Board.

Finally, most nonprofit corporations file an annual report with the Secretary of State's office which reports changes in Trustees and Officers. If you are unclear about whether this is a requirement in your state, call the appropriate agency and find out what form (if any) needs to be filed. At the same time, check with the state Attorney General's office. In some cases a state form similar to Form 990 must be filed.

Rule 8 —
When it comes to money,
BE CAUTIOUS.

Design your budget carefully and conservatively. Be well organized in your bookkeeping and make sure that financial transactions are reviewed periodically by a member of the Board.

Nothing is more important in the administration of a nonprofit organization than proper fiscal management.* Unfortunately, this area is treated too casually by many arts organizations, and sometimes the repercussions are very serious. Too often it is believed that fiscal management is yet another administrative area where goodwill can make up for disorganization. But this is not the case. The threat of a lawsuit or of losing tax-exempt status is very real when there is careless handling of the financial affairs of the organization. Fund raising from public and private sources becomes more difficult if the fiscal credibility of an organization is in doubt. Make sure to keep in mind that management of the financial affairs of even a small nonprofit corporation is very different from handling your personal finances. *You* can probably get away with not balancing your checkbook, not keeping careful records, or not planning a budget; where your personal finances are concerned, no one is likely to bother you. But if you are as casual about the fiscal affairs of your organization, be prepared for trouble.

One of the most important activities of a sponsoring organization is

---

*Two excellent publications on this subject are: *Financial Management for the Arts* by Charles A. Nelson and Frederick J. Turk (American Council for the Arts, 570 Seventh Avenue, New York, New York 10036) and *Museum Accounting Handbook* by William H. Daughtrey, Jr. and Malvern J. Gross, Jr. (American Association of Museums, 1055 Thomas Jefferson Street, NW, Washington, D.C. 20007).

Figure 1

1979 Budget (actual) and 1980 Budget (projected)

RECEIPTS	1979	1980
Ticket Sales	$11,535.50	$13,250.00
Residency Co-Sponsor Income	3,750.00	3,750.00
State Arts Council		1,250.00
Contributions - Individual	3,815.00	4,000.00
Business Firms	2,295.00	2,500.00
Interest on Savings	273.75	275.00
TOTAL RECEIPTS	$21,669.25	$25,025.00
DISBURSEMENTS		
Artists - Touring Companies	$ 9,000.00	$ 9,000.00
In-state performers	3,375.00	5,575.00
Travel to out-of-town performances	75.00	125.00
Lodging for Artists		200.00
TOTAL FOR ARTISTS	12,450.00	14,900.00
Director Fee	4,000.00	4,500.00
Clerical/Typist Fee	600.00	600.00
Scholarship (two given in 1976, one to be given in 1977)	800.00	500.00
Publicity, Printing & Postage	2,480.00	2,800.00
Director's Phone Expenses	280.00	300.00
Rent for Opera House	400.00	800.00
Piano Expense	240.00	240.00
Insurance Premiums	141.00	160.00
Miscellaneous	86.62	100.00
Contingency	191.64	125.00
TOTAL DISBURSEMENTS	$21,669.25	$25,025.00

budgetary planning. To project a budget, you must have a good deal of information at hand concerning anticipated expenses and income. In addition, it is extremely useful to have budgets from previous years. These help establish financial trends and are useful in predicting income and expenditure in each budget category. Figure 1 shows how a projected budget should be lined up next to an actual budget from the previous year. For anyone looking at the proposed budget, the numbers for the same category in the previous year's budget provide the means for verifying what the projected numbers mean relative to actual income and costs. Any increases or decreases must be justified. In the budget laid out in Figure 1, for example, there is a projected increase of almost 15%. However, the executive director was able to justify this increase by demonstrating that an arts council grant would be forthcoming and that

When it comes to money, BE CAUTIOUS.

the two additional events scheduled for the season would bring a minimum of $1,715 in ticket sales.

It is always wise to be conservative in budget projections. The temptation, of course, is to exaggerate anticipated income so that more cash will be available. The inexperienced person will often justify this action by thinking: "If the receipts are not forthcoming, I can always cut expenses. Besides, I am not allowed to show a profit anyway, so it really doesn't matter if we lose a little money."

This kind of thinking is dangerous and shows a fundamental misunderstanding of the nonprofit concept. First, it is difficult to cut spending when one is already well into a season. In most cases, monies are committed well ahead of the time that receipts come in. But more importantly, it is essential that the sponsor think in terms of building up a surplus in good years for reversals in bad. This is *not* considered a profit so long as Board members are not personally enriched by taking the surplus in the form of cash dividends. If the organization plows the surplus directly back into its programs or puts it away in a contingency fund for eventual capital expenditures or future program activities, a surplus is not only legal, it is desirable. An excellent goal is to project modest surpluses each year, until such time as the organization is a full season ahead in receipts and cash on hand. A healthy sponsoring organization is one in which there is enough cash in the bank so that an entire season could take place without income of any kind.

Why preach such fiscal conservatism in an age when organizational growth and development are so popular? Anyone who has seen the devastating effect of rising costs and inflation in the past few years knows that many sponsoring organizations operating "close to the wire" (with nothing put away for contingencies) have disappeared. In addition, growth and development are often only possible when organizations have capital put away for major acquisitions and expenditures (e.g., the renovation of a building or the purchase of a new piano). Many private foundations and public agencies will not commit funds to new projects unless the organization can show a substantial "match" from its own coffers. Thus in a very real sense, on-hand capital attracts money not only in the form of interest on savings, but also in the form of grants and gifts.

Once a budget is approved, the Board is faced with the question of implementation. Who signs checks? Who keep the books? What kind of mechanism is there for monitoring and reviewing the fiscal management? Who makes sure that the monies are being handled legally and properly? Many sponsoring organizations are entirely too casual about such questions. Often an inexperienced administrator with no particular expertise in fiscal management is turned loose with the organization's checkbook. Even with the most well meaning people such a procedure can be disastrous. No one may be able to account for a certain sum of money which has become "lost"; cost overruns in certain categories of the budget may result without anyone being aware that things are remiss. With less scrupulous administrators, the temptation to "borrow" some of the organization's funds may lead to irregularities which cannot be detected or corrected.

In most well-run sponsoring organizations, there are at least two people concerned with fiscal management. One of these is the Treasurer of the corporation, the other, the director or a designate. It is primarily the Treasurer who bears the ultimate responsibility for the proper handling of the organization's money. This is why, in many of the best-run organizations, the Treasurer is in charge of signing checks. Check-signing permits a convenient review of financial transactions and allows the Treasurer the opportunity to verify that the director does not overspend in any budget category without Board approval. It is the director who decides how the organization's appropriated monies are to be spent, and this person must supply the Treasurer with a list of bills to be paid. In some small organizations, particularly those with a small volume of fiscal activity, the director is given the responsibility of signing checks. In these cases it is necessary for the Treasurer to provide some kind of regular review of the books. In no case should one person approve payments, write checks, and review the fiscal activities of the corporation. There are simply too many risks involved — both legal and financial.

In the event that the Treasurer signs checks and the director provides the approved invoices to be paid (a system heartily recommended), the following procedure is quite efficient. The organization invests in a rubber stamp as below:

```
DATE REC'D .................
DATE PAID .................
ACCOUNT   .................
CHECK #   .................
APPROVED  .................
```

When a bill is received, the director stamps it and fills in the first, third, and fifth lines. The first line indicates the date the invoice was received; the third line, the account (or line-item of the budget*) to which the payment should be charged; on the fifth line, the director indicates approval by singing his or her name. The invoice is then forwarded to the Treasurer for payment and lines #2 and #4 are filled in at that time. Later, the invoice is filed for future use if needed. In cases where no invoice or bill is received (as, for example, when performers must be

---

*Each budget category (or line) should be assigned a number (e.g., printing = 101; performer fees = 102; auditorium rental = 103; etc.) to simplify accounting procedures later on. Each time an invoice is processed, the budget category should be referred to by number in the blank marked ''ACCOUNT.'' Each organization's budgetary categories and accounting system should be tailor-made to its particular needs with the assistance of an accountant.

paid), the director merely types a memo in the form of an invoice and treats it as such.

Two observations should be made about the person who signs the checks for the corporation. First, it is a wise precaution for this person to be bonded. Bonding is a form of insurance that protects the organization should the individual do anything improper or illegal. Second, the person who signs checks should also take responsibility for keeping up-to-date accounts of the organization's fiscal activity. The director will need to have cash-flow information and will need periodic reports — either written or oral — on the amounts remaining in the various budget categories. Particularly for a director who does not see the monthly statements from the bank, some form of regular accounting from the Treasurer is essential. For each line of the budget, the Treasurer should indicate the total amount appropriated for the year, the amount already expended, and the amount remaining. If the volume of fiscal activity is heavy, such cash-flow statements should be provided on a monthly basis. For organizations with small budgets, a quarterly or semi-annual statement is usually sufficient.

Conclusion

It is difficult to exaggerate the importance of effective planning, good organization, and responsible fiscal management in the administration of a sponsoring organization. Perhaps it is easiest to underscore the point by stating that funding agencies are at least as concerned about these issues as they are about the artistic merits of your organization. Organizations which are mismanaged are often passed over by these agencies. There is simply too much at stake to risk money on organizations in which administration is not taken seriously.

Many sponsoring organizations justify the casualness of their administrative arrangements on the basis of their small size. "With a budget of less than $4,000, we hardly have to worry about sophisticated questions of management," claims one sponsor. He may be right; one does not need a sledge-hammer to pound a nail, and one probably does not have to worry about very involved administrative issues when the organization's budget is so small. But remember this: no budget is too small to be managed properly; and because sponsoring organizations have a tendency to grow, it is just as well to start off on a sound footing which will allow for safe and well-managed development.

Remember, performers
are PEOPLE too.

Chapter 2
Performers

Rule 9 —
Remember, performers are PEOPLE too.

Senor Pizzicato, the orchestra conductor in the children's classic, *Tubby the Tuba*, is the perfect example of what many people still believe to be the typical performer personality. Aloof, exalted, authoritarian, his accent and foreign origin the very essence of "culture," Senor Pizzicato only moderates his austere personality when meeting people whose musical sensitivity begins to approach his own. We are to be impressed and a little fearful of the maestro, just as we are to be a bit subservient in our dealings with any artist who has chosen to share his performing talents with us.

Unfortunately, the myth of the exalted performer — so charmingly stereotyped for kids in *Tubby the Tuba* — is firmly believed in by many people who must deal with performers on a regular basis. Some performers do foster this image, but, in certain instances, they have been forced into a selfish or arrogant attitude by the insensitivity of audiences and sponsors. "How can I be generous and courteous," asks one, "when on the day of the performance the sponsor keeps phoning, not letting me get any sleep?" "Of course I left the after-concert reception," says another, "I was famished. I hadn't eaten anything before the concert, and all I was offered were some packaged cookies and punch." "I didn't want to appear high-handed," says a third, "but when someone asked me to play the theme from *Doctor Zhivago* during intermission, I asked him to leave the backstage area so I could practice.'' "Six weeks after the performance when I still hadn't received a check,'' says a fourth, "I called the sponsor and got angry. He didn't seem to realize that I had bills to pay too.''

But the fault is not entirely on the side of sponsors and audiences. Performers often exploit the idea that creative people need not fulfill normal obligations or maintain certain minimal levels of courtesy. Some break contracts, occasionally only days before a performance. Others fail to send promotional materials in time to be useful. Still others send a description of the program several weeks ahead, allow this material to be advertised — and then show up with an entirely different program. In addition, sponsors are often expected to suffer quietly when performers make unreasonable demands for their own personal comfort, are tardy for performances, and are rude to members of the audience or committee. In many cases, sponsors feel themselves in an extremely vulnerable position. There is, after all, a performance at stake and they want to do everything in their power to make that performance a success. Nor are they always certain what demands are reasonable. On the theory that it is better to be taken advantage of than to be discourteous, sponsors often give in when they should not.

In the following chapter, an attempt will be made to replace mythology with reality. Sponsor obligations to performers will be detailed, as will the responsibilities of performers to the sponsor. One theme will be consistently stressed: performers are people too. This means that they must be treated like people and must be held responsible like people.

Rule 10 —
DON'T buy a pig in a poke.

Be sure to use more than advertising and promotional materials to verify the quality of the performers you plan to hire.

Hiring performers is a tricky business. One must first attempt to find out how good they are artistically; then it is necessary to try to determine whether they are trustworthy — whether they will honor contracts, be prompt for performances, and, in general, fulfill obligations. Even if all these things check out, there is still the question of whether the group will please the audience. If the performers are doing a residency*, the questions multiply: how effective is the group with young people, in informal settings, in less than ideal performing spaces; is the group adaptable and flexible; will the performers be effective "missionaries" for the arts; will they be courteous?

How can a sponsor determine the answers to all these questions? There is no official reporting and evaluating system which is reliable. Promotional materials, designed to sell the performing group, can be misleading. Even reviews and letters of support are not dependable. A

---

*Cf. p. 45.

DON'T buy
a pig in a poke.

performing group may be using an impressive review in 1977 that was written in 1950. Obviously, much may have changed in the intervening years, but the banner review is still used to entice the unsuspecting sponsor.

The best way to judge performers is to see or hear them in action. Get a list of the group's performing dates in your area. Do not commit yourself as to which performance you are coming to, and do not introduce yourself when you arrive. If your plans include a residency, try to attend at least one workshop or performance with children. Have the performers made an effort to design something special for children or have they simply diluted their adult show? Judge the audience reaction objectively whether or not you personally like the group. If you like what you see, talk to the sponsor. Has the group been prompt for performances? Have the performers been courteous and easy to work with? Have there been any special problems? Ask the sponsor how much he or she paid for the group. This may turn out to be quite important when you start your own negotiations.

Suppose you do not have time to attend a number of performances but want to have the opportunity to see several groups. If you are lucky, there may be a showcase of performing groups in your area in which several performers will be doing short segments of their work for potential sponsors. One way to find out about showcases is to write or call your state arts council. Often this organization sponsors or co-sponsors showcases or can tell you when special showcases may be taking place.

The disadvantage of a showcase is that it is an artificial situation geared toward selling. It is usually not an actual performance before a regular audience. The best showcases attempt to correct this defect by bringing in audiences. One children's theatre showcase in Vermont, for example, took place in a regional high school. Children were brought in from surrounding elementary schools. The sponsors in the audience then had a chance to gauge how successful the performing groups were with children of various ages.

Whether or not you attend a showcase, it is always desirable to speak to sponsors who have hired the specific performing group that you are considering. Ask the booking agent or representative to send you a list of organizations that the group has performed for in the past two years with the name, address, and phone number of each sponsor. Even if the performing group does not send you a complete list and manages to delete the sponsors who would give you the most negative evaluations, you will still receive much valuable information from sponsors who were, on the whole, pleased with the group's work. You will be told what to watch out for, what to insist upon, how much to pay, and other details that will help you not only in making the initial decision but also in dealing with the group later on.

Do not underestimate the importance of performer selection. The reputation of your organization is at stake every time you choose performers. If the group you have chosen presents a mediocre performance, the audience will believe that your organization lacks people with expertise and good judgement. No matter what the previous track record of the organization, one fiasco can do considerable harm to the sponsoring organization's reputation. So be very careful and take the necessary steps to be sure you are buying quality.

Finally, if you have good luck with certain performers, do not be afraid to hire them again. If you are worried about variety, skip a season before re-engaging the group; but remember that many performing groups vary their presentations from year to year anyway. The finest performing groups — those that have built a solid reputation in the field of touring — usually depend on re-engagements for 50 to 75% of their bookings. Nor is this surprising. Reliability and a good track record are precisely what the experienced sponsor is usually looking for.

Rule 11 —
It's often NEGOTIABLE.

The price of a performing group, like the price of a car, can usually be negotiated. Attempt to block-book or arrange a residency, and you will probably see a dramatic drop in price.

If you go to a department store to buy a piece of furniture or an article of clothing, you do not expect to haggle about prices. Occasionally a desired item may be on sale, but you, the purchaser, had little to do with the mark-down. Shopping in a department store is a take-it-or-leave-it situation. Either you buy at the price marked or you do not buy at all.

While there are a handful of star performers or performing groups who fit into the "take-it-or-leave-it" category, most do not; and prices are often adjusted to accommodate special and not-so-special situations. Most performers have a stated fee but this is often open to negotiation. Sponsors should investigate carefully and perhaps bargain a bit before agreeing on a price.

The situation in which a performing group is least likely to lower its fee is when a sponsoring organization wants to hire the group for a single performance in a geographically isolated area. When much travel is involved and there is only a single fee in the offing, the performing group may be unable to lower its fee without losing money. However, the same sponsor who found the group's booking agent firm about price regarding a single performance may find a changed attitude when several performances are possible. After all, the group must pay its performers the same fee for rehearsal and travel whether they do one performance or three. Thus the extra events are "gravy," and the booking agent may reduce the performance fee by 20 to 30% in order to arrange the extra employment.

There are two methods of arranging multiple performances: the block-book and the residency. To block-book, two or more sponsors in the same geographical area cooperate in hiring a performing group. If one sponsor books the group on Monday, the second signs them up for

It's often NEGOTIABLE.

Tuesday. If, in addition, one of the sponsors agrees to house and feed the performers, the fee is lowered by a greater amount. Because the block-booking format can realize such tremendous savings, sponsoring organizations in many parts of the country have developed formal or informal buying consortiums. The members of the consortium cooperate in planning their respective seasons. When they are ready to negotiate with the performing group, they generally can offer multiple bookings and can insist on significantly lower fees. While some consortiums, like the one at the State University of New York in Albany, are actual organizational entities with paid professional staff serving a large membership, many sponsors realize the same benefits simply by keeping in touch by phone with other sponsoring organizations in their area. Says one arts administrator: "Once you pick up the phone and call a colleague about his or her plans for the coming season, you have a consortium; if the two of you can work together, you will usually find that considerable funds can be saved." To find out more about potential cooperating sponsors in your area, get in touch with your state arts council. This organization should have a list of sponsoring organizations in your state and region.

The second method of arranging multiple performances is to organize a residency.* When a performing group does a residency, the performers come into an area for a certain period of time (usually two to five days) and give several formal and informal performances in various community locations — schools, civic clubs, community centers, senior citizen residences, concert halls. The longer the performing group stays, the lower the cost per day. For example, one classical music duo in New England charges $500 for a single performance but only $300/day for a four-day residency which includes three services per day! The savings are dramatic if the sponsoring organization can find other co-sponsors to help defray the total cost of the residency program.

Obviously, if you decide to organize a residency, you must be particularly careful in your choice of the performing group. Many performers who do marvelous work in a concert hall or theatre do poor residencies. They may be unsuccessful with children, stand-offish in informal settings, and generally temperamental in situations which require flexibility and tolerance. It is always advisable to find out, for example, what the minimum requirements for performing space will be *before* the group arrives. Some groups are willing to perform anywhere; others have stringent requirements. Since residency locations vary enormously and have a way of not quite turning out as expected, opt for the more flexible group.

---

*Arranging and carrying out a residency can be a highly complicated affair, particularly when schools are involved. A recent book to guide sponsors and performers through the planning and implementation of school residencies is *The Arts Go To School* (available from the American Council for the Arts, 570 Seventh Avenue, New York, NY 10018).

If the sponsoring organization can provide hospitality (housing and meals for the performing group) during the residency, more money can be saved. But keep the following in mind. Performers need rest; if they are housed in private homes, it should be understood that they are not to be disturbed at certain hours. In addition, many performers have special eating habits. Most do not, for example, like to eat a heavy dinner before a performance. Make sure that the host and hostess are aware of this and do not plan a big dinner party in honor of the invited guests — unless, of course, it is after the performances.

One hospitality system which works well is to house the performers with families, but arrange for meal coupons to be donated by local restaurants. This allows the performers to eat when they want and what they want without being rude to the host families. Sometimes motels or local colleges will donate rooms where the performers can be housed. However, since one of the principle purposes of a residency is to break down the barriers between the performing artist and members of the community, many sponsors prefer the arrangement in which performers stay in private homes.

Finally, with regard to performing group fees, be straight-forward with booking agents when you talk with them. If the fee for a particular group is quoted at $1,000 and you only want to spend $800, ask the booking agent whether there is some way that the group can meet your price. Tell him that your budget is fixed and you will have to book in another group if he cannot meet your price. Very often, compromises can be worked out: if you, for example, will be flexible about a date, the booking agent may arrange an ''en route'' fee when the performing group is in your area anyway. Sponsors have a good deal of leverage when it comes to establishing fees; it is an advantage that few of them use effectively in their dealings with performing groups.

Rule 12 —
INSIST on a contract.

A contract protects the sponsor as much as it does the performing group. Always insist on one and always read it carefully before signing.*

There are some sponsoring organizations which take pride in the fact that they never use contracts with the performing groups they hire. ''We have a special relationship with our performers,'' says one sponsor, ''so why should we risk spoiling it by introducing something as imper-

---

*The standard reference book on this subject is Joseph Golden's *On the Dotted Line: The Anatomy of a Contract,* distributed by the American Council for the Arts, 570 Seventh Avenue, New York, NY 10018. Though many provisions of the contracts described will only be relevant to larger sponsors, any sponsor will glean much useful information from this book.

INSIST
on a contract.

sonal as a contract?'' This attitude is admirable but dangerous. Contracts help to spell out in writing the precise agreement between the performing group and the sponsoring organization. They help prevent misunderstandings or forgetfulness on the part of either signer. A contract should be regarded as a form of insurance for both the performing group and the sponsoring organization.

Some people resist contracts because they are afraid of getting entangled in a legally binding agreement. With small fee contracts, however, litigation is an option which is practically never considered. No one goes to court to collect a $500 fee, just as no sponsoring organization goes to court over a change in the specified number of performers appearing on stage. Neveretheless, a contract serves as a reminder that certain agreements have been made and that either party has a claim on the other if the terms are not met. When either the sponsors or the performers believe they have been short-changed, the contract serves as a document of arbitration. Thus, if you are told by a performing group that they do not use contracts, insist on one (some sample contracts can be found in Appendix B). If you follow the format of contracts that have stood the test of time, you are more likely to have a trouble-free performance or residency.

In looking over a contract sent to you by a performing group, be particularly sensitive to anything which looks unfamiliar or is difficult to understand. Look carefully at ''riders'' — extra pages specifying additional agreements which go beyond those spelled out in the contract proper. Do not sign until you understand all the terms completely. Otherwise, you may be committing yourself to additional costs and responsibilities. For example, in the Master Contract Sample in Appendix B, Rider B, in particular, could spell disaster for a sponsor who initialled it without knowing what was involved. The first paragraph commits the sponsoring organization to as much as $1,000 in additional expenses for a full-sized theatrical company travelling with a union, or ''yellow card'' crew.* If the performance is to take place in a gymnasium, the technical requirements spelled out in the section on lighting toward the bottom of the page could pose insurmountable problems.** It is true that these provisions will rarely be found in contracts used by small groups, but sponsors should always be on the lookout for terms which

---

*When considering a large company, particularly a theatre, ballet, or opera group, always ask if the company is a ''yellow card'' show. If it is, your local union will have jurisdiction over the company's ''call'' for extra stage help and you, the sponsor, will probably be expected to pay the union bill. Whether or not the company is union, be sure you know the extent of extra charges for stagehands before you sign the contract.

**For the sponsor who would like a primer on technical details of performing spaces, the Western States Arts Foundations has published M. Kay Barrell's *The Technical Production Handbook* (1976). Copies can be ordered from the Foundation at 428 East 11th Street, Denver, Colorado 80203.

they are unable or unwilling to meet.

In general, once a contract is signed, it is put away in a file and never referred to again. If there is a disagreement between the sponsors and the performers, however, the contract may provide a useful vehicle for resolution. The contract has a psychological value as well. Once people commit their names to a legal document, they are more likely to be careful in carrying out their responsibilities.

It is true that a contract can never cover every possible contingency. When something happens that is not covered by a contract, the experienced groups tend to compromise. Consider the following example:

A touring opera company was to perform on an evening in February at a university town in western Massachusetts. During the day, a severe snow storm had caused the roads to ice up; and the company trailer truck, carrying the scenery, costumes, lights, and other equipment, jack-knifed two miles from the theatre. There was no hope of getting the truck out of the ditch until the following morning. The performers arrived safely about an hour later. The company manager quickly assessed the situation and determined that it was possible to give a performance since the essential equipment could be taken by pick-up truck to the theatre. Nevertheless, much of the scenery and all of the costumes (which were packed in the front of the truck's trailer) would have to be left behind. A hasty meeting was called with the sponsor, who wanted to postpone the show. The company manager explained that this was impossible: the company was headed to the Midwest the following morning and would not return to New England during the tour. The sponsor countered by saying that he was worried about the size of the audience — the snow might keep them away — and the disappointment of some who had expected to see full scenery and costumes. At this point, the manager made an offer. The company would do the show in street clothes and partial scenery; the conductor would make a special announcement before the performance and explain the scenic situation before each act. If, at the end, the sponsor felt compromised, either artistically or economically, a fair financial settlement could be worked out. The sponsor somewhat reluctantly agreed.

At 8:20 that evening, twenty minutes behind schedule, the performance began with a speech by the conductor to the large audience that had braved the weather and come to the show. By the end of the evening, the audience gave the performers a standing ovation. As one individual said later, "I felt that I was almost a part of the company and that the performers had made a secret pact with us that this was going to be a very special evening." After it was all over, the sponsor decided not to press for any special financial settlement as long as the performing group would pay the stagehands who had appeared for work but had been sent home.

This example shows that when two experienced professionals are willing to compromise, both can turn out to be winners in what otherwise might prove to be a financially calamitous venture.

Utilize your performers FULLY.

Rule 13 —
Utilize your performers FULLY.

Make good use of the performers while they are in your employ. If your organization is truly serving the community, the performers should appear in places where many different people can enjoy them.

One misconception associated with the mystique of the exalted performing artist is that he appears only on an elegant concert stage or in a theatre. There is still a pervasive belief that artists should not be asked to perform in less formal settings. This belief is unfortunate since it prevents sponsors from using performers in places where they might have a marked effect on appreciative audiences. Two national service organizations which have been working hard to combat this situation over the years are Young Audiences and Affiliate Artists. The first has become famous for introducing school-age children to music; the second for saturating communities with informal "noncerts" where distinguished artists perform in every kind of location for diverse audiences.

While the achievements of these organizations are considerable, this should not obscure the fact that much of what they have accomplished can also be done by small, community-based sponsoring organizations. Taking performers to the community does involve careful planning and is certainly more complicated than having the community come to a central location like a concert hall or theatre. Nevertheless, a series of formal performances in an auditorium may prove to be forbidding to people who are not in the habit of attending cultural events; nor will outside funding sources be convinced that sufficiently diverse segments of the population are being served by such a series of programs. Finally, remember the mathematics of performer fees: the longer a group's period of residence, the lower the per-performance fee. If a group is in your area anyway, it is likely that they will be willing to perform one or two extra informal services for a small additional fee.

The most obvious alternate location for performing arts events, and the one most commonly used, is a school auditorium. Since school children are "audiences of the future," they must be cultivated through an exposure to live performances. But sponsors and performers should realize that a standard, 45-minute assembly program before a large group of children may not be the most effective performing format. Intensive sessions with smaller groups should be considered. A brass quintet might do a workshop with high school band players; a puppeteer might work with an art class on puppet construction; dancers might do a session on movement with the physical education class. Not only do these intensive sessions seem to have a longer-lasting effect on children than the more formal assembly programs, but performers generally prefer them. They are less strenuous and more fulfilling. Because of this, many performers will increase their daily time commitment to the sponsoring organization if they are working only with small groups of children (thirty or less). The following example provides an interesting illustration:

> The booking agent for a woodwind quintet doing a residency in a small New England city told the sponsor that she could schedule the group for up to three services each day. For the first two days of the five-day residency, the sponsor organized six large auditorium concerts for elementary school children in various parts of the city. After the second day, the leader of the group told the sponsor that the performers preferred working with fewer children and would be willing to increase the number of services if they could work with individual classrooms. Would she be willing, he asked, to allow the members of the group to split up and make several classroom visits covering an entire school of twenty-one classrooms in a morning? The sponsor agreed and decided to follow one of the musicians — the flutist — on his round of visits. In the first classroom, the performer introduced himself, played a short piece on the flute, then on the piccolo. Afterwards he demonstrated the principle of changing the pitch on wind instruments by means of a coke bottle and colored water. He asked one of the children to "tune" his coke bottle by pouring water to the correct level. Next, the flutist took out a special screwdriver and took apart the flute's foot-joint in order to explain the nature of the instrument's construction. "The instrument is like a very delicately constructed machine," he explained, and then showed what was necessary to keep it in good playing order. During the short question period that followed, there were several queries about the way instruments are put together — this in a town where many parents worked in construction trades. The flutist ended with a spirited flute solo before departing for another classroom.

It is interesting to note in this example that, though the musicians spent an entire morning in the school, the sponsoring organization was only charged for two services.

In considering other community locations for performances, it is best to consult first with the booking agent or leader of the group to find out the minimal requirements for performing space (e.g., dancers generally require a wood floor and will not dance on cement; a renaissance chamber group cannot be heard in a large gymnasium and may request smaller performing spaces). Once you have an idea of space requirements, determine which particular audiences your organization wants to reach. If it is senior citizens, find out whether there is a community facility in which large numbers of older people tend to congregate during the week. If it is the business community, perhaps you should arrange a luncheon performance at one of the civic clubs in town such as the Rotary. Finally, do not be afraid to schedule the performers in shopping centers, banks, factories, or anywhere else where positive exposure to the performing arts will result. Check out your local contacts carefully, however, and make sure you will receive plenty of assistance when you arrive with your group. Someone who has an official connection with the performing space should agree to share responsibility for organizing

PREPARE your performers.

FLIGHT SCHEDULE

INCOMING FLIGHTS

	ARRIVING
CHICAGO	9:45
NEW YORK CITY	11:15
ISTANBUL	10:08
MILWAU...	1:15
SA...	3:35
	4:11
	5:05
	6:10
	6:49
	8:15
	10:06

BAGGAGE CHECK

the special event.

The following is an example of an unusual use of a performing group:

A community-based sponsoring organization which offered several residencies in its city each year was concerned that an entire segment of the population was not being reached. An analysis of audiences revealed that except for college-affiliated individuals, almost no one in the eighteen to thirty-year-old age bracket was attending any of the events. After much deliberation, the program director met with an executive of a large insurance office in the city and asked whether there was any way that he might arrange a program for the clerical workers in his employ, most of whom were women in the desired age range. After some hesitations about the feasibility of the project, the executive suggested that an informal concert be arranged during the mid-afternoon coffee break in the cafeteria. The company, as its contribution, would make the necessary arrangements and allow the coffee break to be stretched to 35 minutes. At 3:15 on a January afternoon, over 300 women filed into the cafeteria, went through the coffee line, and sat quietly as they were treated to an informal performance. For many, it was their first exposure to live music.

In scheduling these extra performances by the group you have selected, keep in mind that there is a limit to the amount of work you can reasonably expect performers to do well. Try to schedule a block of time for performances and another one for the performers to rest. This is generally more desirable than spreading the services throughout the day. You should always find out from the booking agent just how many services you are entitled to and avoid the temptation of increasing this number. If certain members of the group are particularly energetic and enthusiastic and are willing to do additional short appearances on the radio or for potential contributors, you may make use of this opportunity. But do not in any case try to force performers to do more than you have hired them to do.

Occasionally you will find performers who are disdainful of performing in any facility other than a concert hall or a theatre. For them, the residency format is merely a necessary evil in the difficult business of trying to make a living. Try to screen out performers of this type before you hire them; certainly make very clear, before any contract is signed, what plans you have for the group. If you have been detailed and explicit, the group should have few surprises; and you, in turn, should feel you have every right to see your plans carried out.

Rule 14 —
PREPARE your performers.

Be in touch with the performers well before they are expected to arrive. Anticipate any special needs of the group. Give clear information about where they are to go and who will be there to greet them.

A trouble-free event or series of events often depends on the effectiveness of communication between the sponsor and the performing group. Much important information must be exchanged before the performers arrive. Let us assume, for example, that a performing group is coming in for a single evening event, plans to eat in a restaurant, and will be staying in a motel afterwards. About three weeks beforehand, the sponsor can write a note to the leader of the group confirming the date, time, and location of the performance, giving travel directions to a good restaurant and to the auditorium (preferably with a map), and recommending two or more motels in the area with locations and room prices. If, on the other hand, the performers are staying with families, the letter should give the name of the host family where each performer is staying (including children's names), the address, and any other special information which might turn out to be useful (e.g., "the Smiths' daughter, Susan, plays clarinet so I put your clarinetist with them"). In the letter, specify what time you would like the group to arrive and give the name and phone number of two individuals to be called upon arrival (in case one is out, the second can serve as an alternate). Ask for any additional information relevant to the performance (e.g., will music stands be required? will the auditorium be needed for a rehearsal? would the performers be willing to attend a reception after the event? etc.).

If the performing group is involved in a residency which involves several performance locations, it will be necessary to add several items to the letter you send to the leader of the group: a master schedule with the date, time, and location of each performance, a sponsor contact (person to be notified upon arrival) for each performance location, a master map showing the location of restaurants, motel and/or host family homes, and the place where each event is to occur.

One successful community-based organization which specializes in arranging residencies each year has devised the following system for preparatory materials. The usual letter is sent to the performing group's leader three weeks before the date of arrival. Then, when the group arrives, each performer gets an information packet which includes a letter of welcome, a brochure describing the organization's residency programs, an annotated map, and a listing of all essential details concerning the location and time of each performance, information on host families, restaurant coupons, etc. For large performing groups, the same packet of materials can be given to the company manager who will take responsibility for getting the company to the right place at the right time.

It is important to keep in mind that the efforts expended on preparatory work of this kind will have a beneficial effect. With detailed information, performers are less likely to become confused about what is expected of them. Given a sponsor who is on top of things and has attempted to make life a little simpler for them, the performers generally go out of their way to be helpful and supportive.

Be a good PARENT to your performers.

Rule 15 —
Be a good PARENT to your performers.

The care and feeding of performers involves a healthy mix of firmness, fairness, and consistency. Be aware of your obligations but insist on what is your due.

It is impossible to generalize about the behavior of performers. Like any large group of people, those in the performing arts display every kind of personality. Some are kind, helpful, and cooperative; others, unpleasant, self-centered, and difficult to handle. Some performers are extremely nervous; others calm no matter what the situation. The most important thing to remember about performers is that their behavior cannot be predicted simply by their profession. A creative person may be responsible or irresponsible, organized or disorganized, sensitive or insensitive. For this reason, sponsors must assess the personalities of performers on an individual basis and adjust their behavior accordingly.

There are certain things a sponsor should consistently attempt to do for the performers. Many sponsors do not realize, for example, that it is important to praise a job well done. Performers need positive feedback on their work, and this is something that busy sponsors tend to forget. Sponsors should also see to it that performers have adequate time to rest and relax; that they are encouraged to get in some recreational activities while they are in town (one travelling woodwind quintet is famous for two of its members who like to work out every day in a gymnasium); that they have the opportunity to eat well according to their own desired schedule. Sponsors should make sure that there is someone at every performance location to help members of the group find their way around, set up, locate rest rooms, and generally feel welcome; if necessary, someone from the sponsoring organization should offer to lead members of the group to performance locations or, alternately, to drive them to the various performances if they so desire. Finally, it is the sponsor's obligation to pay the performing group promptly after the final performance or service. A check should be handed to the leader of the group before the performers leave town. After all, once the performing group has fulfilled its obligations to your organization, there is no reason why they should be kept waiting for payment. For many performers, a delay in payment can create difficulties with landlords, bill collectors, and the like. If the sponsoring organization is unable to pay on the evening of the final performance, the booking agent or the leader of the group should be told well before the performers' arrival.

Sponsors often assume that performers like to be entertained at parties after performances. While this is often true, it is not always the case. Some performers like to unwind after a couple of hours of hard work on stage; others are tired and want to go to bed; still others want to go off together and have a beer or a quiet evening alone. This is not to say that you should avoid after-performance entertainment; simply that you should clear your plans with the performers and never assume that they should or must come. If you do entertain them after a performance, expect them to be hungry and thirsty. Do not serve them packaged cookies and punch even if that is what you are giving the rest of the guests. Assume that they will want to eat a meal and feed them properly. In many cases, this will be the first real meal of the day for them.

Just as sponsors should make every effort to treat performers well, they have every right to expect performers to meet their obligations to the sponsoring organization. Sponsors should not tolerate a rude or arrogant attitude toward the audience or members of the community. Much harm can be done if the performers do not make a minimal effort to be courteous. If you observe rude behavior, speak to the people involved and explain how important it is for your organization to project a positive image in the community. Ask for their cooperation. Do not get angry but be quite clear about your complaint. As a general rule, tell the group that you expect them to show up twenty minutes to half an hour before the scheduled time of performance. If anyone is late, wait until after the performance is over, and then speak individually to the person involved. Calmly state that you are serious about the twenty minute or half hour "call" and you hope that the lateness was simply an oversight.

Conclusion

Dealing with performers is simple as long as you can combine the wisdom of Solomon, the patience of Job, and the strength of Samson. For most of us, this is an unlikely possibility. As a result, the relationship between sponsors and performers is brought off successfully only when both sides are willing to make an effort. Certainly sponsors can determine to a large extent how things will go. It is sponsors who initially choose performing groups, make the necessary preparatory arrangements, set up schedules, and, in general, establish the tone of the relationship. Sponsors who are flighty, disorganized, unduly harsh, or ridiculously gushing, will not command the respect of performers. Performers do seem to admire sponsors who are well organized, concerned for their comfort, and clear about the requirements of the sponsoring organization.

It is interesting to note that there are many performers who have themselves become successful sponsors. One, who is much respected by the performers he hires, attributes his success to an understanding of the performers' point-of-view. "I always try to put myself in their shoes," he says, "because I remember so clearly my own frustration with sponsors. Perhaps the most important thing to keep in mind is the notion that performers have the same human qualities and frailties as the rest of us."

You have to
MAKE it happen.

Chapter 3
Filling the Auditorium

Rule 16 —
You have to MAKE it happen.

Always assume that the auditorium will be empty unless you have done something about filling it.

There is nothing quite as pathetic as an empty auditorium on a performance night. Not only is it depressing for the performers, but it usually indicates a financial calamity for the organizers of the event. Conversely, there is nothing more uplifting (spiritually and fiscally) than a sold-out hall. There is a special kind of excitement for performers, audience, and management when all seats are filled at performance time.

What magical secret does the successful manager possess which enables him to sell out a hall? Some people claim that the secret is in hiring a big-name attraction or performer, but this is not necessarily true. (I remember a story my grandmother used to tell about attending a concert in Florida featuring Jascha Heifitz; there were only 27 people in a 3,000-seat auditorium.) The secret of successful selling, very simply stated, is hard work. It is true that big names can make the job of selling easier. But much work will be required nonetheless. Potential ticket buyers must somehow find out that a performance is going to take place; once they find out, they must be convinced that they should attend. Visibility is only part of the battle (and selling tickets should be regarded as nothing less than waging war); actually selling the tickets will be the result of personal solicitations, mailings, telephone campaigns, and more.

The issue is whether (to continue our warfare analogy) the manager-general has enough committee-member-troops at his disposal, has mobilized them effectively, has organized their activities in the proper sequence, and has the authority, patience, and presence of mind to make sure that every planned maneuver goes off like clockwork. In the following pages, some of the proven effective tactics will be described. Carried out faithfully, they may well lead to the happiest of outcomes — the enemy, the recalcitrant public, beating down the door of the auditorium trying to gain entrance!

Rule 17 — Check the COMPETITION.

Your first move should be to clear the dates of your events so that they do not conflict with church choir rehearsals, civic club meetings, or other forms of nightly entertainment.

It is truly astounding how much goes on in cities and towns. For the manager of a performing arts sponsorship organization, this fact is often learned the hard way. No sooner are the dates for performances selected and announced than a number of potential ticket buyers start "explaining" why they will not be able to be there. "I must go to recorder group" — ". . . to my Tuesday night choir rehearsal (I've never missed it in seventeen years)" — ". . . to the Altrusa Club meeting (didn't you know that we always meet on the first Tuesday of the month?)" — ". . . to the high school basketball play-off" — and so it goes. Occasionally, of course, these explanations are polite excuses by people who never intended to come to your events anyway; but often, they are legitimate.

Clearing dates is not easy. In fact, there will always be conflicts, and some must be taken more seriously than others. If most of the music lovers in town belong to the church choir, then it is foolhardy to schedule a concert on rehearsal night. Members of your committee should discuss dates with various people in town who are up on local activities. Be sure to check with the chamber of commerce, with churches, schools and other nonprofit organizations to find out what events are already planned for the coming season. Once dates have been selected for the organization's own events, efforts must be made to get the word out to other groups before they schedule competing events for the same times.

One of the best ways to insure that other events will not be planned for the nights you desire for your performances is to work toward a consistent schedule which becomes known around town. If you have one event a month, try to have it fall on the same day (the second Tuesday of every month, for example). If you have an event every week, it should be on the same day and should always begin at the same time.

Once people begin to realize your consistency in scheduling, they will

Check the
COMPETITION.

try to avoid the dates you generally use. Just as you know that Rotary meets every Thursday at 1:00, so the Rotarians will come to know that Tuesday night is concert night in town. If possible, your promotional materials should state this plainly: "Molto Music Presents Eight Tuesday Evenings of Chamber Music." Make the day selection consistent, and your audience will habitually reserve your time slot as they plan their activities for the week or month.

Rule 18 —
Start your subscription
campaign EARLY.

A ticket to a series of events is called a subscription. Selling subscriptions is an extremely effective way to sell tickets. If five events are planned, selling a single subscription is equivalent to selling five individual tickets except that it involves only a fraction of the work. A great advantage of subscription selling is that it brings in large amounts of cash early in the season when money may be desperately needed. In addition, successful subscription selling is usually an indication that there will be a good box office on performance night. There is no reliable rule of thumb to determine whether or not your subscription campaign is going well or is lagging. In certain communities and for certain audiences, a great number of subscriptions will be sold, accounting for perhaps 75% of the seats in the house. In other cases, most tickets will be sold at the door as singles on performance night. One successful concert organization in Maine whose hall has a 400-seat capacity has found that if the auditorium is 25% sold with subscriptions one week before the first concert, most of the series events will be sold-out. While this formula is not necessarily true for every organization, it is useful to analyze subscription sales relative to total ticket sales in order to project a realistic goal for the ticket committee at the beginning of each season.

Subscription selling should begin early — not less than six weeks before the first scheduled performance. While it is possible to offer a discount to the ticket buyer who is willing to buy a subscription, it is usually not a good idea. Keep in mind that people who buy subscriptions are generally the well-to-do who care less about saving $.50 or $1.00 on a ticket and more about seat location or public recognition in the program. For this reason, it is common to ask subscribers to contribute a little extra to the organization by becoming sponsors or patrons. Special benefits can be offered, as described in the section on sponsor/patron selling in the chapter on fund raising.*

Whether you are attempting to attract sponsor/patrons or merely trying to sell subscriptions, direct solicitation by phone is always effective. For the would-be purchaser, it is more difficult to say "no" or to post-

*Cf. p. 91.

pone a decision when a friend or acquaintance is waiting on the other end of the line. The ticket committee can divide up the list of potential buyers, with each person taking the responsibility for phoning several names on the list. If Mrs. Smith knows fifteen individuals on the list, these should be the people she calls. In the case of potential ticket buyers no one knows personally, committee members who live close by should do the calling, perhaps introducing themselves as neighbors who themselves have enjoyed the activities of the organization.

After a number of seasons, as the organization becomes known in the community and the region, it becomes less important to sell subscriptions by phone. Many of the subscribers will be "repeaters" — people who bought subscriptions the year before and are just as likely to respond to a mailing. The phone can still be used for follow-up ("We noticed that you have not bought your subscription this year, and we would like to know whether you want us to reserve the same seat for you that you had last season") or to reach new people who are potential first-time sponsors.

While more will be said about promotional materials later in the chapter, it is important to insert a word here about the kinds of materials that should be sent to would-be subscribers. Generally, these people want to know as much as possible about the upcoming season. A letter describing your plans is essential but is not enough. With the letter you should enclose an attractive brochure and a return envelope in which an order blank and check can be inserted. The brochure should give the details of each event — date, time, performers, program — and should have some pertinent biographical material on the performers. Some successful concert organizations, for example, send a flyer which, when unfolded, includes a listing of all the programs for the season on one side of the sheet. Many subscribers will attach this sheet to a bulletin board as a reminder; the concert association can use extra flyers in other sorts of promotional activity.

Rule 19 — Write EXCITING promotional copy.

If you want your publicity to be most effective, make sure you get promotional materials from the performers well before you think you may need them. If a group is to perform in April, but your flyer must come out in October, make sure the group is aware that you need their materials in August. If they are sending you additional items to promote the performance itself, these should be sent five weeks beforehand to be useful. At the very least, you should receive photographs and some written material which includes biographical data and excerpts from reviews. Occasionally the group will have its own press kit which will include press releases, ad slicks, and dialogue for radio spots. This is

Start your subscription campaign EARLY.

not generally the case, however, and you must assume that the group will not send anything unless you constantly remind the booking agent.

Do not assume that the written material that will be sent to you will be usable in the form in which you receive it. Many fine performing groups send badly written press releases or, worse yet, a set of "biographies." You, or someone from your organization, will have to rework this material into a form which will be sufficiently engaging and interesting whether it is used in the promotional brochure or in a press release.

Finding someone (either paid or volunteer) who will write effective promotional copy should be a top priority task for your organization. An exciting press release is more likely to be used by a newspaper than one which is poorly written; once used, it is more likely to attract an audience. Lively prose in the promotional brochure will also help in selling tickets. The person selected to write should be familiar with the kind of information that people expect to see in descriptions of performing groups. There should be a healthy mix of biographical information, reviews, listings of major cities where the group was well received, information on the selection of works to be performed, etc. The writing itself should be clear and enthusiastic, but always concise.

In writing for the press or for your organization's promotional use, you must always think in terms of selling a product rather than merely announcing an event. To do so, appeal to something analogous to the "objective index of quality" so commonly used by advertisers. For most people, good reviews in major newspapers serve this function; to a lesser degree, a tour itinerary to foreign cities or major cities in the United States indicates that the performing group is probably of high caliber; finally, a testimonial from a celebrity — preferably a performer in the same field — is helpful in establishing the credibility of the performing group.

When you receive the promotional materials from the group, look through them for these items. If you do not find what you want, write back to the booking agent and request specific material. Very often, performers have what you want but will not send it unless asked. All too often they send a list of their teachers or of institutions where members of the group studied. While this may be very impressive to fellow performers, it generally means nothing to most readers — readers who will come to the performance only if they spot something that interests them.

Finally, do not despair if you cannot get adequate promotional materials from the performers. You do not have to write about them. There are always other newsworthy alternatives. After announcing the upcoming event, structure your story around some other news: the recent grant from the state arts council, the after-concert reception, the new piano your organization just purchased. The essential information about the performance will still be contained in the first paragraph and those who read on will be treated to an interesting story.

Rule 20 —
Work CLOSELY with newspapers. *

Work with local, regional, and state-wide newspapers. A loyal newspaper can be a promotional person's best friend.

Despite the growing importance of television and the wide appeal of radio, newspapers still provide the most practical and economical method of getting information about your events to potential ticket buyers. By printing your press releases and agreeing to write feature stories, the newspaper is providing free advertising which reaches a great number of people. In addition, it is usually advisable, if the organization can afford it, to pay for some advertising space in a newspaper.

The logical time to advertise is during the campaign to sell subscriptions (before the season begins) and during the week before each individual event. If your first event is to take place on October 1st, you may well want to run a large ad in the middle of September which lists the dates, performers, and programs for each event and which includes a cut-out coupon that can be sent in as a ticket order form. You can also run a small ad on the day of each event reminding readers where tickets may be purchased. If you are located near a college or university, consider advertising in the campus paper; the rates are usually a bargain.

Most newspapers will help you design your ads. If the performing group supplies ad slicks, the newspaper will add local information about the time and place of the event. If you plan to design your own ad, provide the newspaper with a basic design and the exact typed information to be included. For visual variety, you can use your organization's logo — excellent for establishing an identity — or a photograph of the performing group. In general, do not fill the ad with a lot of prose. Rather, include eye-catching visuals and a minimum of type. Be sure to incorporate large, bold type either to identify your organization and/or performing group or to point out something special about the event (e.g., "A Few Tickets Still Available;" "Special Mime Show Tonight;" "Reduced Prices for Students and Senior Citizens").**

The press release sent to newspapers is an excellent form of free advertising (for a sample press release, cf. Appendix C). Releases should be sent, along with a photograph, to any newspaper that conceivably might print them. Try to find out which editor or department should receive your release and try to develop a personal relationship with the

---

*An excellent reference work is Ted Klein and Fred Danzig's *How to be Heard: Making the Media Work for You* (1974) published by Macmillan Publishing Corporation.

**Occasionally, a local business concern can be encouraged to buy a joint advertisement in which the business is identified as a culturally enlightened enterprise and the upcoming performance is announced and promoted. For more about such an arrangement, cf. p. 96.

Write EXCITING
promotional copy.

person who regularly handles your copy. The release should be typed on plain white paper or the organization's stationery. It should be double or triple-spaced with ample margins. At the top left, type the name, address, and phone of your organization plus the name of a contact person. On the top right, type the date on which you want the story run (e.g., "FOR IMMEDIATE RELEASE: January 15, 1977"). You may want to suggest a headline (if so, keep it short), or you may leave the headline blank. The release should run about 350 words or less. If it runs more than a page, type the word "MORE" at the bottom of the first sheet and type a string of X's at the end of the article. The photo that you send along with the story should include a short identifying caption on the back. Only send photographs with good contrast. Do not send ones that are too dark or diffuse.

Since a newspaper is in the business of printing news, the press release must read as a news story. The first paragraph should begin with the vital statistics on the event (day, time, location, performing group, sponsoring organization, place where tickets can be bought, etc.). The next paragraph should contain the most exciting material about the event. Sentences, particularly in the beginning, should be short; the content, clear. The philosophy behind these rules is simple. Most readers will scan the article casually, only reading the first couple of paragraphs carefully. In addition, there is no guarantee that the newspaper will use your release in its entirety. It is more than likely that the story will be cut to fit into a certain space. As a general rule, cuts are made from the bottom up. The newspaper staff will usually not take the time to read over the cut article to see if it still makes sense. As a result, the material near the end of your release should be non-essential information conveniently packaged in self-sufficient paragraphs.

The most successful organizations generally flood the newspapers with press releases. Curiously, the newspaper people do not seem to mind. In fact, they often print the stories when space allows. Not only can you send releases about upcoming events, but you can write a news story about anything you consider interesting — the arrival of a distinguished guest performer, the purchase of a new piano, the construction of a new set, or the installation of a new lighting system. Have someone churn out the releases and send them off at the rate of at least one or two per week. It is remarkable just how much media exposure your organization can gain through this method.

At the same time that someone is writing press releases, the organization should be inviting newspaper writers (as well as other media people) to each event. Set aside press tickets and encourage regular reviews. Your audiences like to read about events they have attended and the reviews serve as advertising for those who did not attend. Newspaper and magazine staff writers can also write feature stories. For a newspaper to be convinced to do a feature, you must promise the writer "an exclusive" — that is, you must promise that you will not give the same story to someone else working for a competing publication. Feature stories, which are generally handled carefully by the newspaper writers, are

Work CLOSELY with newspapers.

often run with several pictures and printed in a more prominent location than a press release sent by your organization.

Features tend to be in-depth stories of an organization and its activities. They are less oriented toward announcing upcoming events — though they do contain such news — and more toward a study of the individuals connected with the organization, their motivations, goals, frustrations, hopes. Such stories not only represent a valuable form of exposure at the time they appear, but they become part of the promotional package which the organization presents to its contributors, funding agencies, and other supporters. There is a good deal of work associated with feature stories — interesting the newspaper staff, arranging for interviews and photography sessions — but the effort is usually well worthwhile.

In addition to the feature story, the release, and the paid advertisement, your organization should make use of one more promotional service offered by some newspapers and magazines — the Calendar. The Calendar is a listing of events taking place during a particular week or month. If you send a list of your programs to the proper person or department at the newspaper offices, there is a good chance that each will be listed at the appropriate time. Most Calendars have deadlines which are usually well ahead of the date the listing will be run. For example, a small community-based organization in New England may be able to get listings in the New York Times Summer Calendar, but the deadline for receiving the information is in March. The time differential between deadline and listing is not as extreme for smaller newspapers, but it is usually significant and extensions are almost never granted.

Many state arts agencies also have Calendars which are sent to people and organizations in the state that are most interested in the arts. This is obviously an ideal audience for your promotional campaign and a free listing of this sort should not be passed up.

Rule 21 —
Use the RADIO and TV too.

Use the radio to promote your organization's activities. If you cannot afford to advertise, consider becoming a "star-for-a-day" on radio and TV.

Like newspapers, radio stations offer several options to the organization attempting to promote its activities, including public service announcements, advertising, and the interview/talk-show. In the case of television, only the talk-show format is financially feasible.

A public service announcement is generally part of a listing of community events to take place on a particular day. Some stations call the service a "Community Calendar." Since it is free, it is used by many kinds of community organizations such as church groups, service clubs, the YMCA, and the Boy Scouts. Because the Calendar is not always run during prime time and, because it does not particularly emphasize the

Use the RADIO and TV too.

arts and entertainment, it is often not heard by many of the people you would like to reach. Nevertheless, it is an exposure opportunity which should not be ignored. Call the station and find out when and where your listing should be sent. The deadline is rarely more than a week ahead of the broadcast day, and often the listing can be received as little as a day ahead.

Another form of free advertising is the radio or TV interview. Since the hosts and producers like to interview "personalities" — people who have done exotic and unusual things — you are more likely to have an interesting show if you can take one of the performers along with you. However, this is rarely a prerequisite for getting on the air.

Radio advertising, while expensive, often pays significant returns in ticket sales. A nonprofit organization will sometimes be able to negotiate a special advertising rate. For example, some New Hampshire stations will donate one radio advertisement for each one that the organization pays for. Radio ads (or "spots") are sold on the basis of their length in seconds (e.g., 10, 15, 20, 30, or 60 seconds). Several short "spots" are more desirable than one or two long ones if your main concern is to announce the upcoming event. In writing the material, keep it simple. You might begin with the essential information (date, time, place of the event, and where tickets can be purchased) or you might begin with an enthusiastic statement about the performing group. Whichever format you choose, be sure to repeat the essential information at the end of the ad.

Selecting the radio stations with which your organization should do business is difficult. Much time and money can be wasted if you advertise and are interviewed by a station whose listeners are unlikely to attend your events. Certainly, if your area has good music stations, you should try to arrange some exposure for your organization through them. Their listeners are the audience you are after. At the same time you might call the public TV station in your region and find out whether you and perhaps one of the performers can be interviewed. Your own local radio stations are always a possibility, of course, but you must determine how many potential ticket buyers you will reach by using them.

Rule 22 —
Use publicity materials that look PROFESSIONAL.

Design appealing brochures and posters. Then distribute them widely.

Small community-based sponsoring organizations commonly make two mistakes in their promotional campaigns. First, they attempt to save money in design and printing and often end up with shoddy-looking brochures, posters, and programs; second, once the promotional materials are printed, they are only distributed locally.

Promotional materials that look cheap have an odd effect on their viewers. Instead of the intended effect (''My, how wise of the organization to put its money into programming rather than advertising''), a frequent response is: ''Ah, cheap materials, amateurish organization. They probably present second-rate stuff.''

High-quality promotional materials need not be excessively expensive, particularly if a local artist can be convinced to do some designing in exchange for a couple of subscription tickets. One successful concert organization had a lovely silk screen designed for its program covers about nine seasons ago. It is still being used, printed by volunteers who also print the same design onto posters. A local printer takes the programs and posters after the design has been run off in bright colors; he then prints the necessary black type at a nominal charge.

Many people think that hiring a designer will be prohibitively expensive. Two things must be kept in mind, however. The cost of the designer is often a one-time expense. If you like what he has done for your organization, it can usually be used season after season with only minor changes. A second thing to keep in mind is that though you will have to pay the designer for his services, he can often find ways to save you money. Like an architect, his knowledge of materials and workmen may pay for a considerable portion of his fee. For example, in the spring of 1976, the organization which has published this book, the New England Touring Program, needed a promotional booklet. When the designer was given the specifications for the job he suggested that the dimensions of the booklet be changed slightly to avoid immense amounts of paper waste. In the end, the design fee for the attractive 8'' x 8'' booklet was partially paid for by the savings in paper costs.

Where should your organization begin when the time comes to have promotional materials designed? First, someone should be hired to design an identifying logo or line drawing which can be easily adapted for use on stationery, programs, posters, and flyers. The design should be simple without excessive detail; the designer should stay away from half-tones which are difficult to print. The finished design should show up well on a number of different background colors.

Most successful organizations print stationery, brochures, and posters. As described earlier, if the brochure is properly designed, it can unfold into a promotional flyer to be posted on bulletin boards or taped into windows and on walls. When deciding on the quantity that you will need, remember that most of the cost goes into design, set-up, and press time. The extra copies you order will only be as expensive as the paper they are printed on. For example, the difference in cost between 1,000 and 2,000 brochures may only be 10% of the total original estimate. If you have too many items printed up, there is no harm done and little financial loss. But if you underestimate and you must do a second press run, your costs will be high.

Two colors on a brochure and poster are always desirable. Often one of the colors will be black or something dark for the type, so the designer actually has only a single color to play with for visual effect. If you cannot afford two colors, consider printing the type on colored stock. This often looks more attractive than black on white. As a general rule, large sans serif type should be used on the poster (it is easier to recognize at a distance), while serif type should be used in the brochure (it is more common in passages of continuous text). Stay away from exotic type faces even if a particular one captures your fancy as you are looking through a type specimen catalogue. These so-called "display types" are more difficult to read and are usually associated with sleazier forms of advertising.

Your poster must be printed on heavy paper or cardboard in a standard size large enough to be read at a distance. Simple posters are most effective. Keep the amount of type to a minimum and combine it with some eye-catching visual material printed in a color that is not likely to fade excessively when exposed to continuous sunlight. For some of your events, the performing group may provide you with pre-printed posters and flyers as part of its press kit. A space will be provided where your printer can insert the date, time, and place of the performance. If you cannot afford the added expense of another printing bill, someone may be able to hand letter the necessary information on each poster.

Many organizations at some point face the question of whether it is necessary to print posters and other promotional displays at all. Why not do everything by hand? There are often more than enough volunteers around to do attractive posters in paint, crayon, or magic marker.

If you are considering this option, there is one very simple rule: don't! Posters that are done by hand automatically reflect a lack of professionalism on the part of the sponsoring organization. The following anecdote is a case in point:

During the summer of 1976, I attended a concert in northern New England at the invitation of the concert manager. Everything about the event was handled in a professional manner; the music was superb; the hall was filled. After the concert, I was invited to a reception with some other arts administrators representing various organizations in that state. As I walked in, I heard the following comment made by one of the guests to the manager: "All these years, I never realized what marvelous stuff you do here. I did see your posters, of course, but because they were hand done and were not very professional, I just assumed that I wasn't missing much."

The key phrase in the remark quoted above is "not very professional." It is not that the speaker objected to things made by hand — he himself was wearing a beautiful hand-sewn shirt. It is simply that topflight organizations do not allow their promotional materials to be produced in this fashion.

Finally, once your promotional materials are ready, make a concerted effort to distribute them widely. Do not limit yourself to local outlets. Assume that people will drive an hour or an hour and a half to attend your events. Consult a map and get members of the organization to help you take posters and brochures to every conceivable kind of loca-

Use publicity materials that look PROFESSIONAL.

THE FEDERZEKHNUNGEN TRITET

"See them to believe them." *The Daily Moon*

"A... routine you'll never forget." *anonymous*

"I saw them perform in Madrid and I haven't recovered yet." *J. Shedd, critic, Evening Sun*

tion within a reasonable distance. Be sure that every college and university in the state has received your materials. Distribute to chambers of commerce, tourist information centers, motels, and restaurants. Do not forget your state arts council — your poster may well be displayed on the wall of one of the offices and be seen by potential ticket buyers. In general, when in doubt about whether to send your promotional packet, go ahead and send it. At the worst, your materials will be thrown away. At best, they will attract new customers.

Rule 23 —
In ticket pricing, DEMAND fair market value.

Beware of pricing your tickets too inexpensively. To potential ticket buyers, the price of the ticket is a reflection of what you think the evening's entertainment is worth.

Reflect for a moment on your own thoughts as you look through a price list of performing groups. You probably glance at the name of each group, scan the descriptions, and look closely at the prices. If your eye catches a price which seems high, your first reaction may be: "That group is too expensive for us; I won't bother to read about them." Or, alternately, you may think, "Hmm, these people are pretty expensive. They must be good. Let's see what they have done."

If you are like most people, the second reaction describes what is probably going through your mind. This is the way the psychology of pricing in the performing arts seems to work. When a group is very inexpensive, we, the buyers, are suspicious. When the fee is high, we feel that we are buying good quality. This is one reason why many performing groups experience an increase in the number of bookings when they increase their fees. It does not always work this way, of course, but it happens often enough.

The issue of performing group fees has already been dealt with in the chapter on performers and it is not necessary to go over the same material here. What is important is to point out that the very same pricing psychology that operates on you, the purchaser of performing artists, operates on the person who may buy tickets for your events. If tickets are free or very inexpensive, part of the potential audience may stay home, convinced that the offerings are second-rate. Conversely, if the tickets are moderately expensive, people may assume that your organization is offering high-quality events. Many organizations believe that the way to increase the size of the audience is to lower ticket prices. Time and time again, this turns out not to be true. In fact, it often works the other way: when ticket prices go up, so does the demand for tickets.

The danger, of course, is that only the well-to-do will attend your events if ticket prices are too high. But ask yourself this question: is the reason that less affluent people are not attending because of ticket prices? Many of these non-attenders, who are not buying your $2.00 tickets, are regular movie-goers and do not balk at a $2.75 ticket at the theatre. Perhaps, therefore, it is not price which is keeping them away; it is a lack of interest in the kinds of things you are presenting. Everyone agrees that the broadest possible public should become motivated to attend performing arts events. Everyone agrees that your organization should make a concerted effort to reach as many people as possible. Do not assume, however, that you will be successful in the effort simply by lowering your ticket prices.

There is no question that there will always be some who quite genuinely cannot afford to purchase expensive tickets to a performing arts event. Normally, these people fall into predictable groups: students, senior citizens, families with several children, etc. For each of these target populations, the organization can offer less expensive tickets. Students with a proper I.D. traditionally receive discounts, and the trend is toward offering the same rate to people over the age of 65. For large families, a special group rate can be offered. If the parents buy two tickets at the full price, each child gets admitted for a token fee of 75¢ or at no cost. Remember that there are always a number of ways to make less expensive tickets available without sacrificing income from those who can afford to buy the full-priced tickets.

But this still does not solve the problem of how to develop a broader audience. This problem is a complex one but there are certain procedures which, over time, seem to work. First, begin to consider performing spaces other than concert halls or theatres. It may be possible to have the group perform in schools, in the local libraries, in civic clubs, and even in banks, offices, and stores. Remember that part of the problem is exposure. To many in your community, your organization may appear elitist, serving esoteric entertainment to the chosen few. Break down this image by bringing the performing groups to the community. At each informal event, announce the upcoming evening performance. People may follow up their initial interest by attending, and they will certainly tell their friends about what they saw and heard. Undoubtedly, an excited and satisfied member of the audience will be your most effective form of publicity.

Second, if you want to build a new audience, you must make people feel a part of your organization. Start by inviting a neighbor or acquaintance to a performance as your guest. If the person seems enthusiastic, follow up the invitation with a request for some volunteer help. You might ask someone to help arrange flowers for the stage display. Someone else might be asked to help move the piano on stage before the tuner arrives on concert-day. Would they be interested in bringing some friends to the next event? From these first tentative associations, new members of your audience may become loyal supporters of the organization, not only buying tickets but also helping in a number of ways. Feeling needed, after all, is tremendously satisfying, particularly when you are contributing something of yourself to a worthy cause.

Once a number of new people have become associated with the organization in this fashion, one or two should be invited to serve on the Board. You may be surprised just how helpful they can be in building up the size and variety of your audience. Often these new Board members can reach out to segments of the community that you had never reached before. It is important to remember, however, that it takes a long time to change attendance patterns. Building a new and bigger audience is hard work. Nevertheless, it is work which demands your attention and effort. Audience building, after all, is one form of survival insurance.

Usually tickets for events sponsored by small, community-based performing arts series range from $2 to $6 per event, excluding special patron tickets, on the one hand, or discounted tickets for students and senior citizens on the other. Within this range, a number of systems can be devised for figuring out how much your organization should charge. Two strategies are desirable: first, try to tie ticket prices to expenses — that is, attempt to set a target income from tickets which is based on your costs; and second, get to know the purchasing patterns of your audience and set ticket prices in such a way that you maximize income from ticket-buyers — to put it in other words, offer a range of ticket prices so that those who are willing to spend a generous sum for tickets have the opportunity to do so.

Let us examine each of these strategies in detail. A specific example allows us to appreciate how a successful concert organization has tied ticket prices directly to expenses:

The Molto Music Series, Incorporated sponsors ten events during the year. Total expenses for these events is $21,000 of which $12,000 is paid to performers. The organization manages to raise $7,000 each year from the state arts council, private donors, and local businesses. The balance of $14,000 must come from ticket sales. In the 450-seat auditorium, the organization manages to sell an average of 410 tickets per event but estimates conservatively that 380 tickets per event can safely be counted on during the coming season. Thus, the average price of a ticket must be $3.68 if the organization is going to make expenses.

Now let us look at the manner in which the ticket spread is arrived at:

The organization offers patron subscriptions at $50 and manages to sell 75 of them. Over ten events, the $50 subscription works out to $5/performance which is a net gain of $1.32 over the target figure of $3.68/ticket. Thus the 75 subscriptions that are sold net roughly a supplementary $1,000 which can be credited against discounted tickets in the following fashion. The organization wants to offer student and senior citizen tickets at $1.50 or roughly $2 less than the break-even figure. With $1,000 to credit against this loss, the organization can offer 500 tickets at this price or 50 tickets per event.

The remaining 325 tickets can be offered at two prices — $4.00 for reserved seats and $3.00 for unreserved. There should be approximately the same number of each.

In ticket pricing, DEMAND fair market value.

In the example cited above, we are obviously dealing with a well-established organization in a relatively affluent community. This is reflected not only in the size of the turn-out for each event and in the amount charged for tickets, but also in the cost of performers ($1,200/event on the average). Other organizations can scale down costs and ticket prices and should be realistic about the size of the audience that can be counted on. Nevertheless, the same basic procedures can be used in establishing ticket prices.

Finally, some experienced arts administrators use a slightly different procedure in working through the relationship between expenses and admission prices. Instead of beginning with a fixed cost for performing arts talent, they play with ticket prices first. How much can we charge for tickets, they ask, and how many will we sell? How much income can be expected from total ticket sales? How much of this can be spent for performing artists and how much must go toward other expenses? In answering the final question, the manager knows how much he has available when he plans his season and begins to hire performers.

Rule 24 —
Make the night of the
performance something SPECIAL.

Always capitalize on the fact that attendance at your performances gives people the opportunity to have a night out.

Why do people attend performing arts events? Is it simply because they enjoy music, dance, theatre? Of course not. People like to go out and do something special. It can be fun and relaxing, a chance to see one's friends, an opportunity to be seen in good company. Indeed, performing arts events are *social* events and the most successful sponsors capitalize on this fact in their attempts to fill the auditorium.

One of the most obvious ways to take advantage of the social aspect of performing arts events is to attempt to sell tickets to groups of people who ordinarily do things together. Occasionally, special inducements can be offered when a block sale is negotiated. Large groups, such as the local garden club, church group, dance school, or music conservatory may be convinced to purchase tickets en bloc if they are offered a discount.

Sponsoring organizations can sometimes increase the size of the audience through specific social activities. One of the most popular is the pre-performance party. Several members of the Board (or other friends of the organization) can give cocktail or dinner parties immediately preceding the performance. They can invite some of the regular subscribers, but they should also include a number of people who would not normally attend. Most of the guests will probably go from the party to the performance.

There are other, more elaborate devices for making the evening's en-

Make the night of the performance something SPECIAL.

tertainment something special. Occasionally one of the restaurants in town may be willing to promote a "Concert Dinner" for people holding tickets to the performance. On the evening of the concert, ticket holders are offered a different menu (at a special price) if they come between 5:30 and 6:30 P.M. Alternatively, a restaurant or pub might consent to a similar arrangement for food and/or drink after the event.

After the performance it is common to give a reception for the artists. Since people like to meet performers, the reception can be planned carefully as a way to sell more subscriptions or tickets. Some organizations use the "artist-reception" as one of the incentives for subscribers (one organization calls them "Subscriber Parties"). In other cases, the entire audience is invited to an informal "Meet the Artists" reception in the auditorium immediately following the performance. Publicity materials can stress the fact that anyone who buys a ticket is welcome to attend.

Many sponsors have a tendency to get so involved in artistic and administrative details that they forget the social aspect of attendance at performances. For these sponsors, it is helpful to have a few Board members who can suggest how to make the best use of social opportunities in promoting the events. Underestimating the importance of this effort can be costly.

Conclusion

If this chapter has had one theme it is that filling an auditorium is not simply a matter of hiring big-name talent, being blessed with an arts-conscious community, or being very lucky. All of these things help, of course, but what really counts is the willingness of a group of people to put in many hours of hard work. If these people are not available to your organization, you might just as well close up shop — in the long run you cannot survive. On the other hand, if they are available, you have a good chance of filling your auditorium night after night.

Don't
FANTASIZE.

Chapter 4
Fund Raising

Rule 25 —
Don't FANTASIZE.

Fund raising is hard work, expensive, and time-consuming. The initial task must be to develop a credible argument for support.

Most fund raisers I have talked to admit that they occasionally fantasize about collecting money from wealthy people. One fantasy, which seems almost universal, centers upon a rich and benevolent patron who offers to underwrite an organization's activities and cover all deficits, no strings attached. We may smile as we remind ourselves that twentieth-century Medicis are few and far between; but it is remarkable how many of us indulge in some variation of this fantasy without really being aware of it. Many small organizations, for example, spend hours, days, and weeks searching for major backers, pursuing such large funding sources as wealthy individuals, foundations, or the National Endowment for the Arts. There is nothing wrong, of course, in developing fund-raising strategies for the "big angels." But the bread-and-butter support of small and successful community-based arts organizations comes from a broad range of contributors, most of them modest donors who, collectively, give substantial sums of money. For these organizations, the bulk of unearned income comes from local sources — from individuals, small businesses, municipal agencies — and this funding, by and large, represents ongoing support (that is, support which continues from year to year). Generally speaking, unless an organization can show this kind of support, unless it has cultivated a loyal constituency of donors in the local community, major funding sources are not interested in contributing to the cause.

One of the most important things to keep in mind, whether pursuing the large donor or the small contributor, is that your organization must first formulate a convincing case for support. Determining your "fund-raisability" is a primary and ongoing task. You must develop a kind of perspective towards your project which allows you to pinpoint those specific program areas which are most likely to attract contributors. Do not ask people simply to cover a deficit. Rather, ask them to give toward something new, exciting, and specific. If, for example, you have developed programming for ethnic minorities, if you are about to embark on a restoration project for your arts facility, or if you are thinking of setting up a subsidized ticket program for senior citizens, let potential contributors know about these developments.

A second thing to keep in mind is that your organization must allow plenty of lead time in planning the fund-raising effort. Applications to state and federal agencies have filing deadlines and these are generally many months ahead of the specified project date. The Board of Trustees should always be working one to two years ahead in planning such applications. Lead time is also needed in local fund raising. If individual and business contributors are to be listed in a program, for example, solicitations must be made well ahead of the printer's deadline date. Working ahead of a season gives your organization the additional advantage of collecting money for upcoming events, rather than asking contributors to pick up the deficit for the season already completed.

A third consideration in planning a fund-raising campaign is that it usually costs money to raise money. Whether the costs incurred are for printing letters, hiring additional staff, taking a potential contributor to lunch, or for holding a fund-raising party, cash will usually have to be paid out before the returns come in. In the case of every expenditure, the organization will eventually have to resort to some form of cost-benefit analysis. What are the costs involved in bringing in a certain amount of cash? Should these costs be reduced? Can the take be increased?

The realistic fund raiser, then, is the one who can formulate a convincing case for support, realizes the importance of developing a broad base of local contributors, allows plenty of lead time, and is conscious of the expenses involved in a successful campaign for money. The purpose of this chapter is to provide you with some techniques which may prove helpful in your fund-raising efforts.

Rule 26 —
Keep your OBJECTIVES in sight.

Be sure your fund-raising devices are as lucrative as they are clever.
Have you ever heard about a fund-raising scheme that made you smile or burst out laughing? Chances are you have. There have been in-

numerable gimmicks associated with fund-raising events. From bake sales with proceeds of fifty dollars or less, to lavish media auctions which can net over a hundred thousand dollars, the fund-raising event is an excellent example of where cost-benefit analysis should be applied — and so often is not. Fund-raising events can be tremendously successful. They can attract contributors who might otherwise not consider donating to your organization. They can bring media exposure to the organization through a totally unrelated activity and spread the gospel of your good works throughout the community. Yet far too often, the fund-raising event represents an exhausting and time-consuming effort for its planners and executors — an effort all out of proportion to the amount of cash taken in.

There are a number of devices that have been used quite successfully by arts organizations. These include: fashion shows, antique shows, dinner-dances, cheese and wine parties, house or garden tours, and visits to artists' studios. Occasionally an organization will buy a block of tickets to a concert or play at a reduced rate and then sell the seats to contributors at a higher price (the Boston Pops regularly sells out its hall on this basis). More lavish projects include European tours of art capitals, opera houses, or museums conducted by a distinguished guide. The contributor pays a lump sum which covers all expenses plus a contribution to the sponsoring organization. Less extravagant projects include benefit concerts, open rehearsals, and films. Often a special tribute can be paid to a loyal supporter (either living or dead) by associating his or her name with the event. This encourages friends and relatives to contribute generously and allows the organization a special opportunity to say "thank you."

A fund-raising scheme used by the Philadelphia chapter of Young Audiences provides an interesting example:

An initial mailing went out to all musicians in the Philadelphia area who listed themselves in the amateur chamber music players' book. The letter invited the players to a "Clef Dwellers" party, where they would have the opportunity to dine and play music with professional musicians. On a return mailer, all amateur musicians were asked to indicate their instruments, how well they played (A, B, or C) and specific musical works that they knew and enjoyed. In addition, they were to enclose a check (minimum $10) as a contribution to Young Audiences. When the return mailers were received, volunteer planners met with the professional musicians (who were donating their services) to decide how the amateurs would be divided up. Soon afterwards, a letter was sent to all participants giving them information about where they were to go and what music would be played. The first year the "Clef Dwellers" party involved ten houses. One large home housed all the "C-rated musicians" and was the "Orchestra-House." The other nine houses were for chamber ensembles. Each house had at least two professional musicians charged with overseeing the musical activities. Stands and music were provided; the hostess donated the use of her home and provided dinner. The amateurs had

Keep your OBJECTIVES in sight.

only to bring their instruments and themselves.

The "Clef Dwellers" party was such a success that for two years the organization repeated it as a promotional stunt. It was covered in newspapers and used in the organization's publicity materials; and, by the third year, amateur musicians were appearing from outside the Philadelphia area to participate. The intent of "Clef Dwellers" was to broaden the base of support for Young Audiences, to find new contributors, and to build a more extensive mailing list. In all these areas it was successful.

The experience of Young Audiences indicates that the impetus for planning a fund-raising event need not be solely to raise immediate cash. Often a well-planned activity can identify new contributors while publicizing the activities of the organization to a broader segment of the community. Indeed, through effective follow-up, many of the original "Clef Dweller" participants became regular Young Audiences contributors. Thus, while the initial proceeds from the party were modest, the later payoffs were impressive.

Rule 27 —
Make it EASY to contribute
to your organization.

Since ticket buyers are always likely contributors, convince them to donate when they buy their tickets.

One of the oldest and most successful devices for bringing in additional money each year is to set up several categories of support which will encourage ticket buyers to spend more than they have to when they purchase their tickets. In setting up these categories, the organization must decide what special benefits will be offered to encourage participation. Sometimes these benefits are minimal (e.g., the listing of sponsors and patrons in the program). Occasionally the benefits are generous and lavish (e.g., special seats in the auditorium, dinner with the performers, complimentary note paper incorporating the organization's logo, a signed picture of the performers, or free admission to an open rehearsal). In all cases, the organization should maximize income from these categories while minimizing the cost.

Let us take a hypothetical example. An organization plans a series of six events. When ticket subscriptions are offered for the entire series, they will sell for $20. Before they are sold, however, the Board can make a concerted effort to attract special subscribers in three categories as follows:

1. *Contributor:* Contributors buy subscriptions for $60. This entitles them to a special listing on the program, first choice of seats, and an invitation to a special "contributors' reception," to which the performers will also be invited.
2. *Patron:* Patrons buy subscriptions for $35. They are listed in the

program and will be offered their choice of seats before the general mailing to ticket buyers.

3. *Sponsor:* A sponsor pays $25 for a subscription and is listed in the program.

In each of these categories, the buyers can deduct for income-tax purposes a certain sum of money as a contribution. This amount is figured as the price of the special subscription minus the regular subscription price (for instance, the Contributor's deduction would be $60 minus $20, or $40).

While many organizations are content to send out a letter to potential contributors, sponsors, and patrons, it is often the case that the Board of Trustees or the ticket committee will plan a telephone campaign. Without question, this is the most effective way to sell. If a phone campaign is planned, the committee should prepare a list of likely sponsors and divide responsibility for phoning everyone on the list. In addition, two letters should be prepared as follows:

1. Letter #1 goes to people who agree to become sponsors, patrons, or contributors. In addition to saying ''thank you,'' the letter lists the dates of programs, tells where checks should be sent, and asks for special seating requests.

2. Letter #2 goes to people who are unable or unwilling to commit themselves on the phone. Once again, it invites them to buy special subscriptions which are described in the letter. It gives the dates of the programs, additional promotional material (where appropriate), and instructions about where to send checks.

Rule 28 —
Remember your local BUSINESSES.

Too often arts organizations come to believe that attracting funds from businesses involves a major fund-raising effort aimed at one or two large firms. This technique is, more often than not, too costly for the long-term benefits gained. Occasionally a small organization will receive a substantial donation of several thousand dollars from a large, local business concern. But, all too often, the donation is made with the stipulation that it is a one-time gift. Remember that in the business of fund raising, it is the ongoing donors that are the bread-and-butter support of the organization.

A sound approach to developing support is to seek small donations from many businesses in your community. The following is an example of this strategy:

Year #1: The Board of Trustees drew up a list of all local business concerns, and Board members indicated those with whom each had some influence or contact. A donation range was set up; businesses were told they could contribute from $25 to $150 (no more, no less). In exchange they received a special listing in the program. During the first round of soliciting (by personal appointments), thirty businesses

Make it EASY to contribute to your organization.

agreed to participate for a total of $2,500 in contributions. Just before programs went to press, a letter went out to the businesses that had refused to donate the first time they were approached. The letter listed those businesses which would be listed on the program and encouraged the others to participate. After follow-up phone calls, fifteen more checks came in, increasing the total contributions to nearly $4,000. At the end of the season, all participating businesses received thank-you notes with a copy of the program enclosed.

Year #2: All donating businesses from Year #1 received a reminder letter six months before the season started. They were reminded of their contribution from the previous year, given an opportunity to increase it (but only to $150), and told that they could either send their checks immediately or wait until the beginning of the season. The letter ended as follows: "Unless we hear from you, we will assume you will want to be listed again and the printer will be so instructed in preparing his copy." Meanwhile a list was made of other businesses that had not joined up. Specific members of the Board were selected to encourage reluctant business executives. At the end of Year #2, sixty-seven businesses had contributed a total of $5,200.

In commenting on this case history, there are a number of things to bear in mind. First, while the initial work involved was great, the ultimate goal was an ongoing system which required a mailing, a follow-up, and a minimal amount of new solicitation. Once such a system is set up, the support can be counted on year after year. Since the contributor pool is large, some cash will always be coming in, although the amount will fluctuate with business conditions.

Second, there is psychological advantage in setting both a lower and an upper limit to the amount that a small business may contribute. By keeping the lower limit at $25 (which any business can afford), the courtesy $5 or $10 check is eliminated. Yet, by setting the upper limit at $150, business concerns need not feel that the arts organization is expecting a very large gift. Often executives refuse the organization's request, claiming that other community organizations, such as hospitals, the YMCA, Boy Scouts, etc., make substantial demands and receive substantial checks from their businesses. If the arts organization stakes a very modest claim and asks for only $25 to $150, there is usually an increased willingness to participate. After all, by being listed in the program, the business gets credit (at very modest cost) for supporting the cultural life of the community.

Third, the arts organization is in a favorable position when competing businesses are located in the same town. Once one firm elects to make a contribution, the effective fund raiser must not be timid in pointing out to competitors what they are missing by not contributing. The business that has contributed is listed in the program. This tells potential customers in the audience that this public-spirited business supports the community, the arts organization, and the arts in general.

Finally, many local businesses often find themselves short of cash, but are willing to make contributions. In these cases, in-kind contributions

Remember your local BUSINESSES.

can be accepted in lieu of cash. In the example just cited, contributions of flowers and gourmet foods were received. In the case of another organization that had to provide food and housing for musicians, several motels and restaurants donated food and lodging.

There are two other fund-raising techniques which can be effective with local business concerns: underwriting and joint advertising. In underwriting, a business agrees to cover any financial loss on a particular event in exchange for publicity as a joint sponsor. If the event breaks even, the business pays nothing; however, if the cost of the event is $2,000 and only $1,200 is earned through ticket sales, the business-underwriter pays $800, all of which is tax-deductible. In many cases, businesses are willing to serve as underwriters. It gives them a unique opportunity to appear as joint sponsors with minimal risk and effort. For the sponsoring organization, underwriting provides insurance and, often, a sizable contribution.

In addition to underwriting, businesses can offer joint advertising. In such cases, a business concern buys advertising space in the local newspaper, promoting both itself and the activities of the sponsoring organization. In one New England community, for example, the local bank regularly announces upcoming performing arts events in its weekly advertising space. The advertisements project an image of a business enterprise concerned with the cultural affairs of the community. The bank is able to project this image within the limits of the normal advertising budget. Many businesses like this kind of contribution since it costs so little. Sponsoring organizations, in turn, are grateful for the free advertising.

Rule 29 —
Concentrate your efforts
on INDIVIDUAL contributors.

There are two facts that must be kept in mind when an organization decides where time, energy, and money should be expended for the purposes of fund raising. First, individuals contribute far more to charity than all other non-governmental sources combined. More than 75% of the contributions to tax-exempt organizations are made by individuals.* Second, individuals who contribute to nonprofit organizations are not only the very rich. Indeed, about half of the money contributed by individuals comes from people who earn less than $20,000.**

---

*Source: *Filer Commission Report.* (Based on 1974 figures, individuals contributed $26 million or 79% of U.S. total private giving.)

** Source: *Report of the U.S. Census Bureau Survey for Commission on Private Philanthropy and Public Needs,* 1975. (Based on the year 1973, the figures may be somewhat different today, due to the effects of rapid inflation.)

Keeping these two facts in mind, one should observe a number of rules in planning a fund-raising campaign: first, make a concerted effort to solicit funds from individuals; second, develop a variety of fund-raising strategies which will appeal to different types of individuals (incomes vary and so do personal philosophies of philanthropy); and finally, do not dismiss those individuals who are not obviously wealthy (if they are made to believe in your organization and its activities, they could become regular contributors).

To the extent possible, the approach to individuals should be *personal*. In some cases, a member of the Board can take a potential donor to lunch to review the accomplishments of the organization and describe a new project for which funds are needed; in other cases, a personal "P.S." can be added to the form letter which goes out each year to potential contributors. When the appeal is personal, it is much more difficult for the individual being solicited to say "no." For this reason a valuable exercise might be to review all current fund-raising appeals to individuals and see how they could be made more personal. In one case, the organization might convene its entire Board once a year to go over the mailing list of potential donors. Each Board member could pick ten names to solicit personally and twenty names for which a personal handwritten note could be enclosed along with the annual subscription letter. The note might be as simple as the following:

"Dear Jane and Bob,
    I hope you will give some thought to
supporting this fine organization. I think
it is a great asset to the community.
                    Sam"

Alternatively, the note might be more detailed, spelling out quite specifically why Jane and Bob should become contributors. The issue is not so much what is said; it is primarily whether Jane, Bob, and the many others like them, have been convinced that their individual contributions will make a difference. Let us consider some of these forms of individual solicitation in greater detail. A number of important contributors will be solicited personally, and personal letters will go out to others; but it is also usually necessary to send out an annual fund-raising letter to a long list of potential contributors whose donations are expected to be modest (less than $200). The letter can be signed by the Artistic Director of the organization or the President of the Board. It should be short, uncomplicated, and straightforward (a sample fund-raising letter can be found in Appendix D).

Keep in mind that the first sentence or paragraph of the letter will probably determine whether it is thrown in the waste basket or saved for more careful perusal. The letter will not be read carefully in most cases, even if it is saved. Do not go into endless detail. Limit yourself to three or four paragraphs (at most, a typed page). Begin with something clever, humorous, or otherwise engaging and make the appeal quickly and concisely. Do not beat around the bush. Do not pretend that it is not a fund-raising letter. If you do present some particular idea in detail, do so on a separate sheet of paper and refer to this material in the letter. A simple procedure is to refer to two or three accomplishments of the organization in the past year and to mention some specific projects to be undertaken in the upcoming season. You might end with a sentence like the following:

"We hope you will join Mayor Smith and the 207 other contributors who last year helped us to raise a record $5,037 for the ongoing work of our organization."

Along with the letter itself, include a return envelope in which the contributor can enclose a check. Immediately after the individual's check has been received, it must be acknowledged. Here again a personal acknowledgement means a great deal. Someone from the organization should write a short "thank-you" note. A few lines will suffice to convince the contributor that the donation is appreciated.

Since most contributors will want a receipt for income tax purposes, it is desirable to print up some forms as follows:

NAME OF ORGANIZATION
gratefully acknowledges the contribution of

name ....

address ....

....

in the amount of $...

date ....

....

(signed)

If you have these printed on NCR paper (available at a local stationery store), you can keep two duplicate copies for the organization's records. The top sheet, after being filled out, is torn off and a personal "thank-you" note can be written on the back before it is sent off to the donor. One copy can be retained for the treasurer, and the other can go to the fund-raising committee's files.

For contributors who might be willing and able to make sizeable contributions (over $200), personal solicitation is recommended. Here there are no hard-and-fast rules since each potential contributor must be considered as an individual, and the approach to each should be closely tied to what members know of his or her predilections and habits of giving.

In general, a Board member who knows the individual should make an appointment for a personal visit. In certain cases, the artistic director or an articulate performer can sit in on the meeting to describe the program in some detail. The more specific the appeal, the greater the likelihood of success. It is often persuasive to use the following argument: "Five contributors are being asked to donate $300" (toward a specific project); "two have already said yes.' " This gives potential donors some assurance that they are joining in a worthy effort with others. For

Concentrate your efforts
on INDIVIDUAL contributors.

example, here is an actual case history:

> An organization finds that certain repairs have to be made on the interior of the building which they are using for performances. The owner of the building says that he cannot afford to make the improvements, but agrees to let the organization have them done. Estimates come in at $2,652. The organization has $1,000 put aside for capital improvements. State arts councils and the National Endowment for the Arts will not contribute funds for renovations. The fund raising committee meets with the Board and decides to solicit five individuals for $300 each. Two members of the Board agree to make the $300 contribution. Three other people in the community are selected for personal solicitations which three Trustees volunteer to carry out. To each of the meetings, a Board member and the artistic director take photographs of the building as it now looks, a pencil sketch of the improvements, and a copy of the estimate. They explain that $1,600 is already in hand and that two other individuals have agreed to contribute $300 each toward the project. Two of the solicited individuals give $300; one explains that he can give only $100. One more individual is selected and successfully solicited for $300.

Note that in the example cited above, two of the five large donations came from members of the Board of Trustees. In general, Board members must be regarded as primary contributors (as noted in Chapter 1) and should be asked to make a long-term financial commitment to the organization when they are invited to serve. Note also that, in this example, funds were being solicited for what is generally called a "one-time gift." A renovation project is not likely to be repeated for many years, and, for certain individuals this may be very appealing. For others, who are able to make sizeable contributions every year (and most who can give one large gift are financially able to repeat the donation on an annual basis), a different approach should be tried. One successful organization has resorted to the practice of asking ten donors annually for a $275 contribution. The $275 figure was chosen since this is the cost of bringing one guest artist to perform with the resident chamber group. Each contributor is given the option of choosing a guest artist (from a predetermined list) and is encouraged to meet and dine with the performer during the residency period.

Above all, it is essential to keep the obvious in mind — that $200 contributions add up a good deal faster than $10 donations. For example, the statistics for a successful, community-based performing organization in New Hampshire are quite revealing. In 1976, the organization collected $21,000 from 249 individuals. Of this amount, over $17,000 was collected from forty-nine contributors donating between $100 and $1,000. Many of these contributors were Board members who were in the habit of giving large donations year after year. The advice from the fund-raising committee of this organization is as follows:

1. Make a concerted effort to find individuals who can, and will, give $100 or more.

2. Make sure every Board member either gives personally, or can raise, at least $200.
3. Be sure to solicit carefully from every individual who gave $100 or more the year before.
4. Seek to increase the number of contributors in this category by 10% every year.
5. Keep your mailing lists up to date. Check them often and make corrections at least once a year.

Regardless of the approach used, all organizations would agree that once an individual contributes — whether the contribution is large or small — you must give this person the satisfaction of your continued appreciation. Individual contributors must be nurtured so that their donations to your organization become a matter of habit.

Rule 30 —
If you must chase a rainbow,
READ THIS SECTION. *

Undoubtedly the most competitive fund-raising dollars in America are those of the private foundations. There are some 13,000 private foundations in the United States, which collectively give more than 2 billion dollars a year. But of this impressive figure, only about 20 million dollars is spent on the arts. Nor is this the only discouraging statistic. Of the 13,000 private foundations, not more than 600 have paid, professional staffs to review applications carefully. Most of the others are family foundations in which money is awarded on the basis of pet projects at best, or whim, at worst. There is no question that of all the fund-raising marketplaces, the private foundation market is the most competitive.

Competition for dollars is only one issue which must be kept in mind in dealing with private foundations. Another is the issue of artistic compromise. Occasionally artistic compromises must be considered in order to attract funds from any major backer, but this is particularly true when dealing with private foundations. Consider the following example:

An arts organization's chief fund raiser had finally succeeded in getting a luncheon date with a foundation president. During the course of the lunch, the fund raiser described the organization's activities and financial need. The foundation man listened politely, but with obvious disinterest. After dessert he said, ''Have you ever thought about including music students with the professionals in your chamber music concerts? Our foundation is very interested in education. You know, if you were to come in with an application for a perfor-

---

*Much valuable information on foundations can be provided by the Foundation Center, 888 Seventh Avenue, New York, New York 10019, which has produced several excellent publications.

If you must chase a rainbow, READ THIS SECTION.

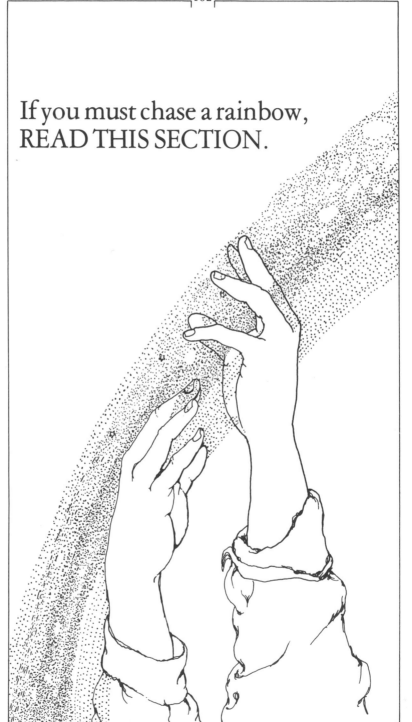

mance which included students and professionals together, I think we might be interested in helping you."

The above conversation poses a dilemma. Clearly, money is being offered, but there are strings attached. And the conditions which have been laid down could have an impact on the artistic integrity of the organization. The foundation representative is not to blame for laying down conditions — he has, in fact, been generous in giving an honest statement about what he can, and cannot, fund. If the sacrifices and compromises necessary are unacceptable, seek money elsewhere.

In soliciting from private foundations, there are certain rules to follow. Only seek money for a specific project; do not ask for funds to support the ongoing work of the organization. Do not send in a formal application until someone from your organization has spoken to a foundation representative personally. Foundations are flooded with appeals and they generally send polite refusals to all those who request through the mail with no advance notice. Before talking with a representative from the foundation, try to find out about its funding guidelines. Modify your request as much as possible to satisfy these guidelines. If possible, try to get an officer of the foundation to review a draft of your application before it is formally submitted. In this way, changes which will increase your chances of success can be incorporated into the final draft. The request itself should consist of the following:

1. a short cover letter on the organization's stationery stating that the enclosed material represents a formal request for funds (the letter should be signed by the Board President or Treasurer).
2. a *one-page* narrative description of the organization and the specific project (if detail is required, put it in supporting documents and refer to these additional "riders" in the narrative description).
3. a proposed budget.
4. supporting documents including programs, press material, and a more detailed description of the project if necessary.

The most common mistakes made by organizations in applying to private foundations are:

1. xeroxing up many copies of a project proposal and sending these to a large number of foundations which have been found in a reference book like the *Foundation Directory* (this method is guaranteed to fail; instead, pick one or two foundations on which to concentrate and try to arrange a meeting between a Board member of your organization and a foundation executive).
2. writing a too detailed or confused application (the clarity of the one-page narrative description and the credibility of the budget are of utmost importance. If detail is needed, you will be asked to supply it later).

If you are successful in receiving funds from a private foundation, be sure to mention this fact in your publicity and your programs. In addition, make an effort to keep the foundation people informed of your activities. Do not assume that foundation executives do not wish to be thanked personally. The organization should show its gratitude publicly (in publicity) and privately (by letter), whether or not it intends to seek funds from this source again.

Rule 31 — When dealing with public funding agencies, PERSEVERE.

Be persistent in asserting your rights as a citizen when you approach public funding agencies. But remember, there are many other citizens!

In the early years of public funding for the arts (from 1965 to the early 1970's), the thrust of the funding guidelines of state and federal agencies favored new or rapidly expanding arts organizations. Unless existing organizations could come up with new and exotic projects, state arts councils and the National Endowment for the Arts regarded them as lower priorities. This policy was not entirely the decision of the administrators dispensing these funds. Congress and the various state legislatures that had appropriated the funds made it quite clear that public money was not to be used to replace contributions from the private sector. There was a great fear that established arts organizations would use whatever political clout they had at their disposal to make themselves richer, more successful, and less reliant on individual and business contributors. The pressure was on the public funding agencies to prove that the taxpayers' money was being used to extend arts activities to various deprived geographical areas and to citizens who might not otherwise have been exposed to the arts.

Today the emphasis seems to be changing and money is now available — especially from state arts councils — for ongoing activities of high quality. Many things have not changed, however. Applications are still submitted on a "project" basis which means that there is no category of support which is simply for continued operating expenses. Also, old priorities favoring projects in rural areas or for arts-deprived clientele in the inner city still apply. Nevertheless, for an established arts organization it is no longer essential to dream up special activities in order to qualify for grants. Financial assistance will be given to high quality arts organizations who can demonstrate an ability to raise money from the private sector and can show a legitimate need. A small arts organization should attempt to establish an ongoing relationship with its state arts council. Indeed this is one of the most promising sources of continuing support.

In order to apply to state arts councils (also called commissions or state arts agencies), one must be familiar with the various programs through which grants can be awarded. Most councils have a document with a title such as "Guide to Programs" which gives the necessary program information together with application deadline dates and other pertinent facts. Read this material carefully before drafting a preliminary proposal-application. Before you submit an application, attempt to get an appointment with someone at the council. Invite this person to an event that your organization is sponsoring. If this is not possible, go to the council and ask for advice. It is important that the council staff get to know you, your organization, and its work. Be persistent. It is your right as a citizen and taxpayer. Remember that you have a greater claim on employees of a public agency than you do on officers of private foundations. Be courteous but firm. Ask for advice and follow it to the extent possible. If your application is turned down the first time, call the council and try to find out why. Ask for help in designing another application. Do not get discouraged. Many organizations that are turned down initially have more success with their state arts agency the next time they apply.

There are several things to keep in mind in applying to a state arts council. First, the council is a government agency funded by federal and state tax revenues. As such, it is subject to the concerns of legislators and taxpayers and must be careful to show that it is not an elitist organization. It is therefore incumbent upon you to show in your application that your organization attempts to serve your entire community. If part of your program is directed toward schoolchildren, senior citizens, or handicapped people, be sure to emphasize this in your application. If you have a specific project directed toward inner-city neighborhoods or rural settlements, perhaps this is the one for which you should be seeking funds. By doing so, you help the arts administrator justify the agency to the legislators and, ultimately, to the taxpayer.

Second, keep in mind that the administrator's name with which you are probably most familiar is the council's executive director. Because this person is the titular head of the agency, it might seem logical to attempt to get an appointment with him or her. However, the executive director generally has a very full schedule and often is not the person administering the specific program under which you are applying. You are frequently better off getting an appointment with a specific program administrator who can give you more time and can provide you with detailed information about your application.

Third, in filling out the application, be clear, concise, accurate, and brief. Remember that as a public agency, a state council is required to review every application it receives. The volume of requests is tremendous. Applications that are bogged down with detail or are confusing stand a very good chance of being set aside. Applications in which the numbers do not add up correctly will not receive a favorable reading. If you must include detail or supporting documents, do not attach them to the application itself, but refer to them as "Rider A," "Rider B," etc. If you are given the option of using extra sheets of paper to continue a narrative description of your project, try to avoid doing so. The sheer bulk and length of your application is not an index of its credibility. In fact, it is much more impressive when a major program is cogently summarized — and more than a little frustrating to receive a fistful of programs, clippings, and descriptive prose.

Fourth, do not ignore the fact that many state arts councils can pro-

When dealing with
public funding agencies,
PERSEVERE.

vide your organization with various kinds of technical assistance, particularly in the area of program development. Though the assistance generally involves a contribution of consultant time and services rather than a cash grant, good technical assistance can be extremely valuable. It is not uncommon to receive help in the areas of administration, promotion, and fund raising, for example. Some state arts councils regard this as a primary responsibility to their constituents. Says one executive director: "All too often the state arts agency is cast in the role of fortress-to-be assaulted rather than partner. For some of us, the accent is on problem solving first and dispensing money later — sometimes we find ourselves wrestling clients with dollar signs in their eyes to the mat before getting to talk to them calmly and reasonably about their objectives and overall needs."

Finally, remember your obligation to lobby for your state arts council and for its parent agency, the National Endowment for the Arts. Just as you may be dependent on these organizations for support, so they are dependent on the actions of legislators at the state and national level. Consider it your responsibility to write regularly to your state and national representatives. When government funding has been involved in a project, mention how important the event was in the cultural life of your community. Invite legislators to your own events. Act as an advocate to strengthen the concept of government support for arts projects. Unless you as a citizen show strong support, you as a sponsor will not get the money you want from the state arts council because it will simply not be available.

As almost all readers of this book probably know, the National Endowment for the Arts is an agency of the federal government located in Washington, D.C. and is charged with the responsibility of making grants to organizations concerned with the arts throughout the United States. Established by the U.S. Congress in the mid-1960's, the NEA has grown rapidly and now has a budget of approximately 150 million dollars. As government agencies go, it is small; yet the NEA's impact on the arts in America has been immense. Many small arts organizations probably receive cash or services indirectly from the National Endowment for the Arts without even being aware of it. Program funds for state arts councils come partially from the Endowment; so do administrative funds for numerous arts service organizations. (The publication of this book was made possible in part by a grant from the NEA).

To many arts organizations, the National Endowment for the Arts often seems like a giant monolith, a sprawling bureaucracy. Whether or not this perception is correct, it certainly is true that there is a high level of frustration associated with direct appeals to the NEA for funds, particularly with those sent by organizations with modest budgets. The Endowment is flooded with such applications. Most are turned down. Those that are successful often represent months or years of hard work, planning, and several previous rejections. A small organization should think twice about applying to the National Endowment for the Arts. If an approach to this funding source is to be made, persistence bordering on doggedness is recommended. (A recommended procedure can be found in Appendix E).

Like the state arts councils, the National Endowment for the Arts gives money through certain program areas. Write to the National Endowment for the Arts (Washington, D.C., 20506) and request the publication entitled *Guide to Programs*. Read the book carefully, pencil in hand, marking those programs to which you might apply. Then write again to the NEA requesting the specific booklets describing each of the programs you are interested in. These spell out the guidelines in greater detail and are more useful than the composite guide.

Before you submit your official application to the National Endowment for the Arts, you should be in touch with your area's Regional Representative.* This is an individual who lives in your region and is responsible for making site visits to potential applicants, assisting them in applying, and giving them basic information on how the Endowment works. (You can get the name and address of this person from your state arts council). Though the Regional Representative is not an evaluator as such, you should attempt to make a good impression during his or her visit. Try to arrange things so that the visit will fall on a day when something exciting or important is happening. Keep in mind that Regional Representatives can speak on behalf of organizations when applications are reviewed in Washington and often write field reports for the Endowment staff summarizing their impressions of the site visits.

As with state arts councils, the application to the National Endowment for the Arts should be clear and concise. Do not count on getting a grant. Do not make any commitments based on the expectation that funds will be forthcoming. Expect to be turned down the first time you apply. Remember that the National Endowment for the Arts was not set up primarily to help organizations like yours (this is the responsibility of state arts councils) and will only take an interest in your organization if you have an extremely compelling project.

State arts councils and the National Endowment for the Arts are not the only government agencies which dispense funds to arts organizations. In cities there are a number of agencies, departments, and programs that are potential supporters of a small arts organization. Such agencies include Departments of Education, Community Action Programs, Office of the Mayor, Model Cities Agencies, Human Relations Commissions, Departments of Parks and Recreation. In smaller towns, public libraries, schools, and the Town Office itself should be solicited. (Civic clubs, though not municipal entities, are occasionally a source of funds). Board members who have connections with any of these potential funding sources should make direct, personal solicitations and attempt to get a commitment of continuing support from year to year.

---

*Before submitting your NEA application, consult with your state arts council. Not only can this agency give you help and advice, but it may also serve as an advocate on your behalf if and when the Endowment staff calls the state agency to find out more about your organization.

Conclusion

This chapter began with a description of the fantasy which lurks in the back of every fund raiser's mind: "Somewhere, somehow, I will find someone who is very, very wealthy to support our organization. Somewhere, somehow, I will find a foundation or a government agency which has just been waiting to bestow money on us." In the course of this chapter, I have tried to show how important it is to keep some perspective on that dream. Fund raising, like anything else, does not happen by itself. It is the result of planning carefully, formulating convincing arguments for support, and putting in countless hours of hard work. Successful fund raisers know that their organizations are kept afloat by a large number of loyal contributors — mostly individuals — who donate money year after year. If your organization has not yet achieved such a situation, get busy: there is much work to be done! There is a large potential constituency in your local community. Work on individuals, small businesses, and your state arts council; seek ongoing, dependable relationships with them. If you develop this kind of support, you will weather the economic storms which are the peril of other arts organizations, and you can look forward to many successful seasons.

Don't buy a
RUBE GOLDBERG!

Chapter 5
Behind the Curtain

"Let's have a dance, theatre, or opera company next season. We have always talked about doing something big."

or

"How about an outdoor festival next summer? We could have a 'street theatre' all over town and a special event in the park."

These are familiar words to anyone who has spent much time with a sponsoring organization. There is almost always someone who wants to bring in more ambitious productions or put on performances in outdoor locations. Chamber music or a solo concert is fine, they argue, but it appeals to a narrow group of music lovers. What is really needed is either something grand and elaborate or something outdoors which is fun. For the winter series, these people may suggest a performing group which can attract a large audience — a Balinese dance group, a Gilbert and Sullivan operetta, a Shakespearean theatre troupe... or maybe Verdi's *Aida?* For the summer series, they may urge the selection of a bluegrass band, a children's theatre ensemble, or even a small-scale circus which can perform on the Town Green. The basic argument is simple: such events appeal to a broader audience which makes it easier to raise money and sell tickets.

The argument is not unreasonable but the sponsoring organization must think carefully about two issues: the cost of such events and their mechanical and technical requirements.* Most sponsors are wise enough to ask how much such events will cost, but many do not realize that this

---

*Appendix F has a glossary of technical terms.

question cannot be answered without knowing how much time, effort, and money will have to be expended for equipment and technical staff. They also do not consider the immense drain on time and energy that large indoor or outdoor productions can represent for sponsoring organizations. A large touring company may have many logistical and technical problems which require more expertise, organization, time, and patience than the staff and the Board can spare. Outdoor productions offer many problems, not the least of which is the unpredictability of weather and the additional worries of postponement and/or relocation.

This chapter will be concerned with some of the important technical considerations which help to determine how much time, effort, and money specific kinds of performances require. It will give some advice on how to avoid technical disasters, how to plan for indoor or outdoor extravaganzas, and how to remain calm and confident in the most trying of pre-performance situations. As always, the key requirement is good advance planning and a realistic appraisal of what you and your organization can manage to accomplish.

Rule 32 —
Don't buy a RUBE GOLDBERG!

Let us start with the obvious. If you want to avoid a technical nightmare, you can help yourself immensely by not hiring a performing group which will, by its very nature and complexity, offer a host of insurmountable technical problems. Some large touring productions require very little technical equipment or expertise from sponsors. They are self-contained packages needing only large performing space. Other touring shows — even some which are otherwise remarkably modest — seem like the classic "Rube Goldberg" as far as their technical requirements are concerned. Complex and intricate, they call for a great deal of expertise, labor, and equipment supplied by the sponsoring organization.

How does one avoid these overwhelmingly demanding productions? Obviously, as a first step the sponsoring organization must find out exactly what it is buying. Someone with technical and production knowledge must carefully evaluate the technical responsibilities of the sponsor before a contract is signed. This information is essential regardless of the size of the company or the type of production. Indeed, it is important to point out that almost any touring performer or group will require some technical help. Even a small chamber ensemble will probably require a clean, properly heated stage area, chairs and music stands, a tuned piano, adequate toilet facilities, and a stage manager. When the technical requirements are modest, they may or may not be spelled out in the contract (if you do not find any there, ask the booking agent or a member of the group). With larger touring attractions, technical requirements are almost always spelled out on separate pages called technical "riders" or "spec sheets." Many sponsors initial these riders without understanding what they mean. Don't do it. As always, read the fine print.

A second way to avoid buying a "Rube Goldberg" is to find out whether the large performing group you are considering has done a lot of touring. If it has, ask for a list of other sponsors who have hired the group in the past and find out from them what the costs were, how much equipment had to be supplied, how flexible the performing group's technical people were, how many work-hours the sponsoring organization had to contribute. If the performing group has not done a lot of touring, beware! Never consider performers simply because you have seen them do impressive productions in their own theatre. Touring, particularly the touring of "one-nighters," is a very special kind of operation. Setups must be done in a matter of hours, not days. A local, often inexperienced, crew must be trained without the luxury of many rehearsals. Local equipment may be less than ideal and will vary from night to night. Touring equipment breaks down and must be repaired or replaced. An excellent company without touring experience may be very unrealistic about all these factors when it puts shows on the road for the first time. All too often, the technical staff expects excellent performance facilities and expert crews. The more experienced touring groups know that such expectations are unrealistic.

Finally, if you want to avoid the pitfalls of a technical disaster, keep your end of the bargain. If the stage crew is your responsibility, make sure that the proper number of stagehands is at the auditorium on time. If you have promised to hang some lights before the group arrives, be sure this gets done. The performing group is depending on you. If you meet your obligations, it is more likely that you can keep costs in line and enjoy a trouble-free performance.

The essence of a good relationship between sponsor and performing group involves effective communication. Obviously, this depends on a dialogue in which both sides ask questions and understand what the answers to their questions really mean. In the remaining sections, we will review some of the questions you can expect from the performing group and others that you should be asking in return.

Rule 33 — Know your SPACE.

The first questions you should be prepared to answer concern your performing space. If it is an indoor location, is it a high school auditorium, a church, a concert hall, a theatre, or a gym? Does it have a stage? If so, what kind (e.g., proscenium, thrust, or arena)? What are the stage dimensions? What type of floor does it have? Is there an orchestra pit? What kind of lighting exists? What are the backstage facilities like? Is yours a union house? These are all basic questions which should determine to a large extent what kinds of performing groups you can

Know
your SPACE.

consider.

The type of performing space is important whether you are considering a solo performer or a large company. For example, a recorder soloist needs a relatively small auditorium with good acoustics: a gym would be totally inappropriate. If your facility does not have a stage, do not despair — but choose the performing group carefully. Some touring attractions require only a "four-wall rental" (that is, a large open space with adequate seating and electrical power). They are sufficiently versatile to put on a convincing performance in almost any location. But increasingly, larger companies are becoming more discriminating about where they perform, particularly as the number of adequate performing spaces is increasing.

There are several kinds of stages and you should be familiar with what you have. There are three basic stage types: proscenium, thrust, and arena. The most familiar is the proscenium stage in which the stage area is separated completely from the audience by the proscenium arch and, usually, a curtain. The audience looks at the stage from one direction, and the action on stage is directed through the proscenium opening. A thrust stage is generally surrounded by the audience on two or three sides while an arena stage offers theatre-in-the-round with the audience completely surrounding the stage area.

Most large touring attractions are intended for proscenium stages. Scenery is designed so that the action will play downstage (in front). (This same scenery will block the view of some members of the audience if it is placed on an arena stage.) Stage action is "blocked" so that performers face out and are downstage when important action or lines are required. Lighting is set up so that performers are adequately lit from one direction only — much simpler than having to light adequately for many different audience positions. If backstage activity is vital, if performer exits and entrances are numerous, a proscenium stage, with its backstage area well masked from the audience's view, may be the only kind that the performing group can use. Any sponsoring organization which does not have a proscenium theatre must be sure that the performing group can put on a good show in the space available.

Stage dimensions vary and so do the requirements of touring productions. A large opera group, for example, will probably require *as a minimum* a stage with 25 feet from the back wall to the curtain line, 36 feet in stage width, and no less than 14 feet in stage height. If the group carries an orchestra, it will need a pit area in front of the stage (dimensions vary with the number of players). Dance troupes may be less concerned with stage dimensions and more interested in having an adequate floor. For a dancer, the floor is a part of the performing instrument. It allows the dancer to give the proper physical expression to the body by supplying the proper resilience and slickness. Non-resilient floors like concrete are actually dangerous for dancers, and you must be sure not only that the floor surface is wood but that it is not laid directly over concrete or supported by metal piers which allow no floor movement. If the dance troupe seems particularly worried about your floor surface, put them in touch with a local dancer and have this individual check out the floor carefully according to the company's instructions.

In addition to the stage area, the performing group will require adequate backstage facilities. Again, this applies as much to a solo performer as it does to a large group, although the exact needs of each may differ. A backstage area without a toilet is a hardship, and many contracts require both a toilet, and a sink with hot and cold running water. A large troupe will also require dressing rooms. In gymnasiums, locker rooms are often adequate if they are near the stage area and have no public access during the performance. Some groups are flexible and will work with what you have. But be sure to tell them what to expect before they arrive and, preferably, before you sign the contract.

There are numerous other items that a large company will have to check out before it arrives. Often, these items are covered in a questionnaire that the more experienced groups send out as a matter of course.* These questionnaires should be taken very seriously. If they are filled out accurately and completely, the technical staff of the company can evaluate your particular setup in great detail *before* the group arrives. If the company does not send a questionnaire, be sure to volunteer as much information about your space as possible. A performing group is almost always under a severe time pressure when a setup is involved, and the company's technical people should not have to discover the idiosyncrasies of your space after they arrive. If your facility has a "technical director," let this person handle the technical liaison with the performing group.

Rule 34 —
For outdoor performances, avoid a DESERT ISLAND or TIMES SQUARE.

Be sure to choose an outdoor space which is neither too isolated nor too noisy.

Outdoor events are the backbone of the summer arts programming of parks and recreation departments and are effectively utilized by other groups who want to take performers to various locations in a particular community. But outdoor performances do offer a host of technical problems, and it is good to think carefully about these in the early stages of planning.

Choosing an outdoor space offers a special set of problems. In choos-

---

*Sample questionnaires can be found in the publications referred to in footnotes on page 14 and 48.

For outdoor performances, avoid a DESERT ISLAND or TIMES SQUARE.

ing a space you must select a location that your potential audience can find easily (try to avoid locations for which detailed directions or maps are necessary). It must have adequate parking nearby, be relatively free of noise and other pollution, and must offer no potential conflicts with others who may have a prior claim upon it. (In this connection, most municipal park departments issue free "park-use" permits.) Downtown open spaces can be checked with City Hall, the Chamber of Commerce, or, in smaller towns, with the Town Manager's Office. Vacant lots must be cleared with their owners, private or public. In all cases you should get written permission which guarantees you certain rights in the use of the space during performance time.

Before making a final decision on your space, estimate carefully the number of people you expect to attend the event. Determine whether there is adequate seating close enough to the performance area so that the audience will be able to see and hear comfortably. Sound diffuses quickly out-of-doors particularly when there is wind, so be conservative about how far performers' voices or instruments will carry without an electrical sound system. You must also determine whether your audience will be seated in chairs, on grass, or be forced to stand during the performance. If the ground around the stage area is not grassy and clean, you should probably provide chairs. If the performance is long, seating is a virtual necessity. However, if your performance is within the context of a festival or bazaar and the audience feels free to come and go, seating need not be provided.

In choosing an outdoor space, containment and traffic flow must also be considered. If admission is charged, entrance locations must be restricted. Many outdoor spaces which are commonly used for paying customers (e.g., fairgrounds, stadiums) are designed carefully with containment in mind. Not only does this assure the elimination of "crashers" (people trying to get in free), but it allows the sponsoring group to control the number of people entering the space at any particular time. This may be particularly important if the space has a legal restriction on capacity. If you are selecting a space which is not designed in this fashion, think carefully about how you can judiciously place barriers and people to control the flow of your audience.

The most skillful outdoor-event planners are fully familiar with every aspect of their space. They work with maps on which they have marked the flow of traffic and people. Often, they also indicate the sun's position and movement so that performance spaces can be set up without the sun blinding either audience or performers (an especially severe problem in the early morning or late afternoon). They know the location of emergency exits, fire hydrants, and other safety equipment. They have figured out the most judicious places to station police and committee representatives. When the event actually takes place, they have a very exact sense of how the space will be utilized throughout the performance period.

Outdoor stages present unique problems which must be worked out ahead of time. Aside from the usual considerations (dimensions, floor, etc.), stages constructed for outdoor events must be tested to make sure they are level and their height must be carefully planned with the eye level of the audience in mind. Stage backing must also be provided both for visual and acoustical reasons. The best backing is an acoustical shell but, should this not be available, you can use fabric to mask off visual distractions behind the stage and to provide maximum sound projection. Be sure to test the background on a windy day to make certain that it is properly anchored. The stage should be placed in a location which is as sheltered from the wind as possible.

The general stage area must be accessible by car and truck if any equipment is to be brought in and there must be secure areas behind the stage to store equipment. If no dressing rooms are close by, think about renting a trailer or enclosed truck which can be parked behind the stage and can be used by the performers. Even if performers do not have costume changes or can be convinced to change into costume at another location, it is desirable to have a portable rest room in back of the stage area for their exclusive use. Off-stage areas on either side of the performing space should be masked off with canvas tarps and ropes so that performers' entrances and exits will be hidden from the audience's view.

Rule 35 — Remember, on every outdoor festival, a little RAIN must fall.

Obviously, nothing will save you from being at the mercy of the heavens, but you can plan for contingencies. In New England, the old saying is, "if you don't like the weather, just wait a minute," and this predictable unpredictability has taught outdoor performance planners to be resourceful. They pick their dates carefully after consulting the weather bureau for long-range forecasts and checking satellite projections, the advice of old-timers, and the *Farmer's Almanac*. They try to avoid hurricane season and are as conservative as possible in deciding when things are going to warm up in the spring and cool down in the fall. Nevertheless, the best planners always assume that their luck in predicting the weather will not last forever, and they take the necessary precautions.

First, they make sure they have plenty of sheets and tarpaulins to protect equipment from rain in case they have misjudged the sky. They use electrical equipment which is water tight. They make sure everything is properly anchored in case of high winds. If the day is clear but windy, they make sure that microphones are equipped with wind shields to prevent "whistling" and that clothespins or clamps are provided with the music stands so that sheet music does not blow away.

Sometimes a downpour makes an outdoor performance out of the question. In such cases, you must either postpone the event or move it to an indoor location. Alternate facilities or rain dates should always be

Remember, on every outdoor festival, a little RAIN must fall.

announced as part of the event's promotion so that the audience knows how to plan. Whatever contingency plans you have made, be sure to make any necessary decision about relocation/postponement early after getting the pre-dawn weather forecasts. As soon as your decision is made, get the word out to performers, committee members, and staff. Have a phoning strategy in mind before the day of the event so that you do not have to waste important setup time contacting people. Someone who is assigned the task of phoning should have handy all the relevant phone numbers including those of local radio stations. The radio is the best way to announce your change of plans to the audience.

For many sponsors of outdoor events, postponement is always preferable to indoor performances. Suitable alternate locations may be unavailable and the entire spirit of the event might be compromised if it is held indoors. In such cases, it is essential that the performing group know precisely what your procedure will be in the case of inclement weather. Include a rider in the contract such as the one below:

Sample Rider

All performances will take place outdoors. In the case of inclement weather the sponsor reserves the right to postpone performances. Postponement decisions will be made by the sponsor at least 6 hours before the scheduled performance, and it will be the responsibility of the performer to make contact with the sponsor before the performance (phone numbers below). A postponed performance will be rescheduled at the convenience of both parties.

If no such rider is included, and if the performing group shows up on the performance day and is ready and willing to put on a show, you may be legally obligated to provide some form of compensation. Certainly, you have a moral obligation to pay performers who have carried out their part of the bargain in good faith. Therefore, be sure that the understanding about contingencies is clear. If you must instruct performers to come "just in case" (particularly if a considerable travel distance is involved), be prepared to pay expenses plus a small honorarium if the event does not come off.

The unpredictability of the weather is not only frustrating; it can be a financial problem. The "just in case" honorarium mentioned above is only one form of expense; others include lost revenues if the day is grey and forbidding, the cost of staff and crew time for postponed performances, the rental of alternate space. Always include a "weather-contingency" line in your budget. It is a sound form of weather insurance.

Rule 36 —
Know the UNION rules.

Many sponsoring organizations decide to put on their gala event in a large, downtown auditorium with plenty of seats; only after the decision is made do they discover that the auditorium is a union house. Often this means unexpected stagehand and musician expenses. Even if the sponsoring group is careful to choose a house over which the various unions do not have direct jurisdiction, the touring group itself may be a union company. If this is the case, local union members will expect to be hired as stagehands and the company will be required to work with them. In addition, "loaders" may show up from the local Teamsters' Union to unload the company's truck.

The best way to avoid union problems is to understand why they occur. There are several unions connected with the performance business and each has its own rules. There are three categories of unions with which the sponsor should be familiar: musicians, stagehands, and loaders. Here is what you should know about each.

Musicians: Most touring instrumentalists belong to the American Federation of Musicians (AFofM) while singers and dancers often belong to the American Guild of Musical Artists (AGMA). In general, neither union will deal directly with the sponsor. However, in certain large, downtown performing spaces, the local office of the American Federation of Musicians may have "jurisdiction": this means that a certain specified number of local union members must be hired for every performance. If no musicians are needed (as in the case of theatrical productions), or if the performing group brings in its own musicians from outside the union local, the sponsoring organization may find that it has to pay "house" musicians from the union local. In certain cases, the sponsoring organization may be able to work out a compromise with the business office of the union but only if negotiations begin before the performing space has been definitely confirmed.

You should also be aware that it is a common procedure for the local office of the AFofM to demand "work dues" from any players from outside the union local who come in to perform and are playing within its jurisdiction. Thus, if you hire a group from out of town, even in an auditorium without "house" musician arrangements, you may see a representative from the local union at performance time. In this case, remember that he is there to speak with the musicians, not with you. Work dues are a local union's tax on players and in no case should you expect to pay them.

Stagehands: One of the most common sources of misunderstandings comes from dealing with the various stagehands' unions. These include IATSE (International Alliance of Theatrical Stage Employees), MPMOUSC (Moving Picture Machine Operators of the United States and Canada), and TWAU (Theatrical Wardrobe Attendants Union). Most touring companies do not carry all of their own technical help and

Know the UNION rules.

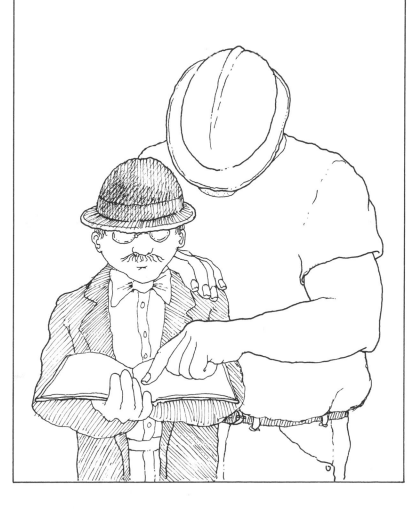

they usually specify that a certain number of local helpers will be needed. In almost every case, it is the sponsoring organization which will have to pay this local crew. For this reason, it is important to get the least expensive crew which can do an adequate job. Often students at a local college are adequate and are certainly much less expensive than union stagehands. The company will specify the amount of expertise and experience that is expected from the local crew. In many cases, strong and willing individuals with very little experience are sufficient.

In some cases, the sponsoring organization will have to hire a union crew, but this is something that should be determined before a contract is signed with the performing group. Obviously, if the sponsoring organization elects to put on the performance in a union-controlled auditorium, local union stagehands will be required. Always ask whether the unions have jurisdiction over a particular theatre before you confirm a rental. If they do, you should try to estimate your stagehand costs carefully. You may find out that you cannot afford the production you have been considering.

Avoiding a union-controlled house does not guarantee that you will not have to hire a union crew. If the stagehands who travel with the performing group are themselves union members, they are required to send out a so-called "yellow card" to the business agent of each local union in whose jurisdiction they will be performing. The "yellow card" announces that their show is coming to your town, gives the time and place of the setup, and requests a certain number of stage carpenters, electricians, people to handle props, etc. If the "yellow card" is sent (and touring union crews *must* send it or face stiff fines), you should expect a full union crew regardless of where the production is going to take place. Clearly, then, one of the most important questions to ask potential touring companies is: are you a "yellow-card" company? If the answer is "yes," be sure to estimate the cost of your union stagehands carefully before signing the contract. Remember, too, that many fine groups are available that travel with nonunion stage help.

Does a "yellow-card" company always work with a local union crew? The preceding paragraph suggests that it does; so do the rules of the stagehands' unions. But in reality, a number of compromise situations have been worked out between local sponsoring organizations and the business agents of small union locals*. If you live in a non-urban area, for example, it is quite likely that the local is small and that most of the members are film projectionists with steady jobs who do not wish to take a night off to work with the incoming group. The business agent may be willing to allow you to hire your own nonunion crew; or, he may suggest that you hire one or two of his workers and fill out the crew with your own nonunion people (students, friends, janitorial staff). Do not assume that the union will be unreasonable. In many cases,

---

*To find the address and phone number of your local IATSE representative, contact the national office at Suite 1900, 1270 Avenue of the Americas, New York City, New York, 10020, 212-245-4369.

workable compromises have been arranged which guarantee the sponsoring organization some very good union help assisted by an inexperienced student crew. But remember that these arrangements must be worked out well ahead of performance day, preferably before a contract is signed with the performing group.

Loaders: According to strict union definitions, stagehands are not supposed to load or unload a truck, although in most cases they do. This work is supposed to be done by loaders who are members of the Teamsters' Union. In many auditoriums around the country, Teamster loaders never appear. But in larger cities and even in some smaller communities, union loaders may be required.

The situations which determine whether or not loaders will appear are very similar to those of union stagehands. They can appear when the auditorium is union controlled; or they may sometimes appear if the touring company's union truck driver sends out a notification to the local Teamsters' office about the company's performance (even if he does, it is not certain that any loaders will appear). If loaders do arrive on the scene, your contract with the performing group will probably specify that your organization must pay them.

The unexpected appearance of loaders can be financially devastating to a sponsoring organization. Not only are their work rates high, but they must often be paid for a certain minimum number of hours regardless of how long they actually work. For example, it is not unheard-of to pay a couple of loaders for a four-hour "in" (unload) and a four-hour "out" (reload) when the work itself only takes 45 minutes each way. Because loader bills can run as much as several hundred dollars, it is essential to know whether they will appear before you make any firm plans to book a particular performing group in a specific theatre.

The easiest way to make sure that you will not have loaders is to hire a nonunion company for a nonunion house. But even if you bring in a "yellow-card" company, the likelihood of loaders is minimal in a nonunion auditorium. Check the contract carefully. See if there is a provision for loaders. If there is, ask the booking agent whether or not the company's truck driver is a Teamster. If he is not, and if you are careful to avoid a union-controlled hall in your area, you will probably not experience any difficulties.

Rule 37 —
Hire RELIABLE technical help.

Many sponsors expend a lot of energy selecting excellent performing groups but are fairly casual about hiring technical help. Their attitude seems to be, "anyone will do." But inadequate technical help can mar an otherwise excellent performance. Consider the following example:

A touring opera company arrives in town with its own staff of four well-trained technicians. A crew of fourteen local people, assembled somewhat haphazardly by the sponsor, is waiting to help them set up and run the show. Among the local crew members are five students. At 1 o'clock in the afternoon they help unload the company truck but at 2:30 they go off to an afternoon class. They return at 5 p.m. Because they have not been a part of the setup, they do not really understand how the scene changes will work during the show and the company's chief technician decides to give them simple jobs which do not require a great deal of explanation. One student is assigned to curtain pulling. However, at 7 p.m. he decides to go out with friends and gets another student to fill in for him. In explaining the curtain cue (a warning light turned on, followed by a curtain-pull light turned off), he gets the instructions reversed. During the performance, 45 seconds before the end of the first act, the warning cue is given but is mistaken for the curtain-pull cue. The curtain closes just before the tenor and soprano sing their final high "C"'s — the most important vocal moment of the entire first act.

While not all examples are so dramatic, others show how important it is to hire responsible and reliable people who will care about the quality of their work. Any experienced touring group can tell you stories about local crews that damaged valuable equipment, talked loudly backstage during the performance, arrived two hours late for setup, or "forgot" that they were responsible for a load-out after the show and walked away with some of the company's equipment instead.

Clearly it is in your interest to hire reliable help. If the local crew is union, you do not have control over who will work. The business agent of the local office will supply the men. In other cases, however, where hiring the crew is your responsibility, take it seriously. Here are some rules you should follow:

1. If your facility has a technical director or building manager, this person should be consulted when a crew is hired and should be paid to be on site during the entire time the company is in residence. If such a person is not available, another individual must be selected who knows where all equipment is stored, has the authority to make decisions, and has keys to every room.

2. If you hire a student crew, be sure that the same students will be available for the entire load-in, setup, and working of the show. (It is permissible to get other individuals for the load-out after the show.)

3. Try not to hire temperamental people for your stage crew (prima donnas belong on the stage, not behind it). The technical staff of the touring group will be under great pressure and should be given willing, cooperative people with whom to work.

4. Make certain that your crew members arrive ON TIME for the crew "call" (the time set for unloading the truck). Nothing is more frustrating than a short crew (fewer people than requested) at precisely the time when many helpers are needed.

5. Find out from the touring group how much technical expertise is needed among your crew members. In many cases you will find

Hire RELIABLE technical help.

that willing and able-bodied novices are suitable. If not, be sure you provide people with the proper technical know-how.

6. If your facility presents special load-in or setup problems, ask the technical representative of the performing group whether the company will require additional local crew members. The performing group is making an assumption that your facility is not out of the ordinary and that load-in and setup will be normal. Some load-ins are not straightforward, however. There are some facilities which require forklifting equipment or carrying scenery up a flight of stairs, for example, and these special situations require either additional helpers or an earlier crew call so that the company's tight setup schedule can be met.

In addition to technical workers, you may have to hire police and firemen. The rules governing the use of your space will probably specify the exact requirements for police and fire protection. Sometimes the expense is borne by the town, in other cases either your organization or the manager of the space must pay the individuals on duty. Regardless of who is responsible for payment, it is a good idea for you to make contact with the police and fire departments ahead of time and, if possible, talk to the individuals who will be present at your event about potential problems.

For indoor facilities, police will probably be most concerned about parking problems and, in certain cases, about unruly behavior in the building. Firemen will be concerned about restricting smoking, keeping fire exits clear, and maintaining the legal limit of people in the building. Go over these requirements and regulations with the individuals on duty. Do not harass them about the rules which they must enforce but rather attempt to work out, in advance, how specific situations (such as an overflow crowd or illegally parked cars) will be handled. Your interest and cooperation will reap great rewards if a troublesome situation requires delicate handling later on.

For outdoor performances, the fire department will be particularly concerned about events which take place near buildings or in tents. Firemen may also need to be on hand if a large number of people is expected to attend or if an event requires a great amount of electrical equipment. Often, however, no firemen will be required for small outdoor events. Regardless of this fact, you should certainly notify the fire department as to the date, time, and location of your event. At the same time, find out whether there are any special regulations which should be enforced. If your event has potential fire hazards of any kind, request a piece of fire apparatus on standby.

Many municipal police departments have a special events bureau which handles large outdoor events; most have police officers with some experience in this area. Once police are assigned to you for an outdoor event, become friendly with them and discuss the procedures which you agree will be most effective for your particular program. Impress upon them that you do not want them to control the crowd, simply to watch over it. Usually it makes sense to station one police officer near the stage area (for security) and another in back of the audience area. You may also want to use police to patrol entrance gates. Because police are expensive, do not hire more than you need and be certain your budget will cover the number you want to hire.

Rule 38 —
Supply proper equipment
that WORKS.

The only way to know what equipment you must supply is to ask the company before you sign the contract. Find out what the power requirements are, how many lighting instruments (lamps, gels, and dimmers) will be needed, how much cable and masking is required, and what type of sound system the company is requesting. Once you have made a commitment to supply equipment, you are obligated to provide items in good working order that correspond closely to the exact specifications given by the company.

In outdoor performance spaces, the power question is especially important. In estimating power needs, remember that outdoor lighting requires a great deal of current and you should evaluate a performing group's technical specifications with this in mind.* If sufficient standing power is unavailable, you will have to resort to generators. These can sometimes be obtained free or for a nominal charge from highway, public works, or fire departments. Generators tend to be noisy and give off unpleasant odors, so a downwind location is a must (the power capability of the generator plus the gauge of the electrical cable will determine just how far from the performing space the machine can be stationed). Generators seem to be temperamental at times and require constant care and fueling. It may be a good idea to station someone near your generator for security and fueling purposes.

Other kinds of equipment, particularly lighting and sound equipment not carried by the performing group, must be borrowed, rented, or purchased. Many sponsoring organizations gradually build up the technical equipment in their auditoriums by purchasing items which can be amortized over several years and many productions. If, for example, there are several shows a month that require amplification, it may be wise to look into the possibility of purchasing an adequate sound system. This is particularly true where the cost of rental is high and equipment is not always easy to find.

In larger cities and towns, theatrical rental houses can supply the

---

*Wherever possible, avoid outdoor performances with complex lighting requirements. Aside from the power problems and the risk to the equipment due to the unpredictability of weather, it is immensely difficult to achieve successful lighting effects outdoors and it requires an electrician with considerable experience and skill.

Supply proper
equipment
that WORKS.

needs of local sponsors needing additional equipment. But there are several things to keep in mind: rental equipment is often not delivered on time, delivery can be quite expensive, and, most important, rental equipment is usually not kept in good repair. It is common, for example, to find essential parts missing from complicated machinery. For all these reasons, the sponsoring organization must check carefully into the reputation of the rental firms it deals with. If there is a local auditorium that has the equipment you need, try borrowing or renting from this source first (you can at least test the equipment and transport it yourself). If, instead, you do end up dealing with a rental firm, have someone with technical expertise check the equipment, and call several times in advance to verify the delivery date and time.

While performing groups will probably specify the equipment they would like to use, most will be flexible if you are unable to supply all of it. Occasionally, one piece of equipment can be substituted for another, or the technical requirements can be simplified or changed. But in fairness to the technical staff, give plenty of advance warning if you are running into difficulties. Do not wait until the company's arrival to inform them that they will not be receiving what they asked you to supply.

Rule 39 —
Be PREPARED.

Be prepared! It's the boy scout's watchword and, from all available evidence, many sponsors were never boy scouts. Ask the technical staff of a touring company what is the most common problem on the road and you will probably be told: "We never seem to get a full crew at the time of the load-in. People do eventually dribble in, but we end up unloading the truck ourselves." If you press the point, you may be told that the second most common problem is having to work with a space which has not been adequately cleared of scenery and debris from an earlier production. Consider the following account:

> The crew call for a touring theatre company setup had been set for 1:00 p.m. at a college in Pennsylvania. The company's truck driver and crew had driven through the night from Ohio, checked in at a motel at 7:00 a.m., got a few hours of sleep, and arrived at the facility at 12:30 p.m. No one was around. The building was locked. Large cans, apparently of trash and debris, were sitting on the loading dock. The sponsor, the head of the college's Humanities Department, was in a class and could not be reached until 2:00. After much searching, someone who had a key let the technical staff into the building. Walking into the facility, the four individuals gazed with horror at the remains of a circus that had been in the building the night before. There were no seats in the auditorium. Equipment was stacked on the stage and backstage. The room was full of paper trash and soft drink bottles. Worst of all, no one seemed to know anything about a local

crew. In desperation, the technical staff attempted to clear the loading dock and unload the company truck. Much to their dismay, they found that the large cans on the dock were filled with animal defecation and that the trash department was not scheduled to clear the area until 4:00 p.m.

It is largely as a result of situations like this one that touring companies have put riders into their contract like the one below:

Sample Rider

The company will carry its own technical staff. The company will request, in advance, additional workers (stagehands, loaders and unloaders) in the numbers required for the setup, performance and strike of the show. In the past this has usually amounted to an additional _____ persons. Local auspices is responsible for paying these workers.

If the number of additional stagehands as specified to the business agent of the local stagehands' union or directly to the auspices is not going to be present at the time of unloading, working the show and loading, the crew of the company will engage additional personnel; and the auspices will be responsible for paying these additional people at $35.00 per person, up to the number specified.

Exactly what does this rider mean? If the company has requested a local crew of 14 at 1:00 p.m., and if only twelve show up, then the technical staff can hire two additional people (members of the company's administrative staff, performers, etc.) and the sponsor will be responsible for paying each of these individuals $35.00 for their work. If the sponsor has not bothered to hire any crew members (and, believe it or not, sometimes this occurs), the company can legally submit a stagehands' bill of $490. Obviously, it is better for both the sponsor and the performing group if a full crew shows up on time and the stage area is cleared and ready for setup.

There are other ways for sponsors to be prepared for the performing group's technical staff. Often sponsors commit themselves to supplying various kinds of sound and lighting equipment. Once this commitment is made, it is necessary to verify that the equipment will be delivered or be available when needed. Do not assume, for example, that just because your auditorium is supplied with the necessary lighting instruments that the performing group will be permitted to use them. Check with the building manager or technical director and get permission to use the equipment; make sure this person is available to answer questions when the technical staff of the company arrives. If equipment is to be delivered to the auditorium, call the supplier several times to verify that it is ordered or has been sent, and make sure that someone is at the auditorium to receive and sign for it.

Being prepared for the performing group also involves making certain that all pre-rigging has been carried out according to the company's instructions before the arrival of the crew. It is quite common, for

Be PREPARED.

example, for a company to send a light plot ahead so that lights can be hung before the official crew call. If the sponsor does not carry out this pre-rigging, the time pressure on the technical staff becomes severe and, in some cases, unpleasant compromises must be made. If a light plot which is totally unworkable in your auditorium is sent to you, call the technical representative of the company immediately. Reasonable changes can be made in plenty of time to get the pre-rigging carried out on schedule. Do not, however, make any changes in the lighting plan or in any other pre-rigging instructions without discussing them with the company representative so that the technical staff should know what to expect upon arrival.

Finally, being prepared for the performing group means being ready to handle any unforeseen complications during the day of the performance. Give the company several telephone numbers to call so that some member of your organization will be available to give immediate answers to specific questions. Even if a company member does not call, go to the auditorium during the morning of the group's arrival to make sure everything is ready. Once the technical staff has arrived and has started to work, return to the auditorium and make sure things are going smoothly. Your interest and help will be appreciated and ultimately may contribute to a trouble-free performance.

Conclusion

Part of the magic of attending a performance as a member of the audience is that one does not know what goes on behind the curtain. In large productions, scenery and lighting changes seem to occur automatically at the proper moments and we can be shifted from a bedroom to a country scene in a matter of minutes. In less lavish productions, even those involving only one or two musicians, we do not see the instrument cases, the street clothes, or the water glasses stored backstage; we are treated to a performance. In a way, this is one of the things that makes a performing arts event so special. Behind the curtain the performers are not out of the ordinary (they are tired or thirsty or worried about the rent check); in front, they become important participants in an event which stretches our imaginations, makes us enlightened, happy, or sad.

This chapter has been called "Behind the Curtain" because the curtain is a somewhat arbitrary barrier between two worlds — the world of lighting equipment, dressing rooms, stagehands, paychecks, and the world of the show. If anyone ought to be aware of the arbitrariness of this barrier, it is the sponsor who must pay attention to both sides of the curtain at all times. Sponsors, after all, must make certain that the show *will* go on. With them rests the ultimate responsibility for all phases of the performance: choosing artistic talent, providing technical back-up, balancing budgets, raising money, promoting the event, and so on. In many cases the sponsor's job is thankless and all the glory seems to go to the performers. But sponsors have the unique opportunity to see both behind the curtain and in front — to observe the magic of the show but at the same time to be in on the secrets of that magic. Perhaps this is why so many of us, despite every kind of setback, complication, and disappointment, continue to find such satisfaction in presenting performances year after year.

Appendices

Appendix A — Sample Bylaws*

Bylaws of Molto Music & Dance Series, Inc.

(A Massachusetts nonprofit corporation)

Section 1. NAME, PURPOSES, LOCATION, CORPORATE SEAL AND FISCAL YEAR

1.1 *Name and Purposes.* The name and purposes of the corporation shall be set forth in the articles of organization.

1.2 *Location.* The principal office of the corporation in the Commonwealth of Massachusetts shall initially be located at the place set forth in the articles of organization of the corporation. The directors may change the location of the principal office in the Commonwealth of Massachusetts effective upon filing a certificate with the Secretary of the Commonwealth.

1.3 *Corporate Seal.* The directors may adopt and alter the seal of the corporation.

1.4 *Fiscal Year.* The fiscal year of the corporation shall, unless otherwise decided by the directors, end June 30 in each year.

Section 2. MEMBERS

The corporation shall have no members.**

Section 3. SPONSORS, BENEFACTORS, CONTRIBUTORS, ADVISORS, FRIENDS OF THE CORPORATION

The directors may designate certain persons or groups of persons as sponsors, benefactors, contributors, advisers or friends of the corporation or such other title as they deem appropriate. Such persons shall serve in an honorary capacity and, except as the directors shall otherwise designate, shall in such capacity have no right to notice of or to vote at any meeting, shall not be considered for purposes of establishing a quorum, and shall have no other rights or responsibilities.

Section 4. BOARD OF DIRECTORS

4.1 *Number, Election, and Tenure.* The number of Directors shall be twenty. At any special or regular meeting the Directors then in office may increase the number of Directors and elect new Directors to complete the number so fixed; or they may decrease the number of Directors but only to eliminate vacancies existing by reason of death, resignation, removal or disqualification of one or more Directors. Each Director shall hold office for a fixed term of one, two, or three years as

---

*Grateful acknowledgement is made to the Massachusetts Continuing Legal Education — New England Law Institute, Inc. which developed the bylaws on which these were patterned.

**Some states may require that the corporation have members.

set by the other Directors at the time of his election. If a Director dies, resigns, is removed, becomes disqualified, or comes to the end of his term, his successor will be elected by a majority of Directors then in office.

4.2 *Powers.* The affairs of the corporation shall be managed by the directors who shall have and may exercise all the powers of the corporation.

4.3 *Committees.* The directors may elect or appoint one or more committees and may delegate to any such committee or committees any or all of their powers. Any committee to which the powers of the directors are delegated shall consist solely of directors. Unless the directors otherwise designate, committees shall conduct their affairs in the same manner as is provided in these bylaws for the directors. The members of any committee shall remain in office at the pleasure of the directors.

4.4 *Suspension or Removal.* A director may be suspended or removed with cause by vote of a majority of the directors then in office. A director may be removed with cause only after reasonable notice and opportunity to be heard.

4.5 *Resignation.* A director may resign by delivering his written resignation to the president, treasurer or clerk of the corporation, to a meeting of directors or to the corporation at its principal office. Such resignation shall be effective upon receipt (unless specified to be effective at some other time) and acceptance thereof shall not be necessary to make it effective unless it so states.

4.6 *Vacancies.* Any vacancy in the board of directors, except a vacancy resulting from enlargement which must be filled in accordance with Section 4.1, may be filled by the directors. Each successor shall hold office for the unexpired term or until he sooner dies, resigns, is removed or becomes disqualified. The directors shall have and may exercise all their powers notwithstanding the existence of one or more vacancies in their number.

4.7 *Annual Meeting.* The annual meeting of the directors shall be held at 12:00 o'clock noon on the fourth Friday in April in each year or if that date is a legal holiday in the place where the meeting is to be held, then at the same hour on the next succeeding day not a legal holiday. The annual meeting may be held at the principal office of the corporation or at such other place within the United States as the president or directors shall determine. Notice of any change of the date fixed in these bylaws for the annual meeting shall be given to all members at least twenty days before the new date fixed for such meeting.

4.8 *Regular Meetings.* Regular meetings of the directors may be held at such places and at such times as the directors may determine.

4.9 *Special Meetings.* Special meetings of the directors may be held at any time and at any place when called by the president or by two or more directors.

4.10 *Call and Notice.*

a. *Regular Meetings.* No call or notice shall be required for regular meetings of directors, provided that reasonable notice of the first regular meeting following the determination by the directors of the times and places for regular meetings shall be given to absent directors, specifying the purpose of a regular meeting shall be given to each director if either contracts or transactions of the corporation with interested persons or amendments to these bylaws are to be considered at the meeting and shall be given as otherwise required by law, the articles of organization or these bylaws.

b. *Special Meetings.* Reasonable notice of the time and place of special meetings of the directors shall be given to each director. Such notice need not specify the purposes of a meeting, unless otherwise required by law, the articles of organization or these bylaws or unless there is to be considered at the meeting contracts or transactions of the corporation with interested persons, amendments to these bylaws, an increase or decrease in the number of directors, or removal or suspension of a director.

c. *Reasonable and Sufficient Notice.* Except as otherwise expressly provided, it shall be reasonable and sufficient notice to a director to send notice by mail at least forty-eight hours or by telegram at least twenty-four hours before the meeting addressed to him at his usual or last known business or residence address or to give notice to him in person or by telephone at least twenty-four hours before the meeting.

d. *Waiver of Notice.* Whenever notice of a meeting is required, such notice need not be given to any director if a written waiver of notice, executed by him (or his attorney thereunto authorized) before or after the meeting, is filed with the records of the meeting, or to any director who attends the meeting without protesting prior thereto or at its commencement the lack of notice to him. A waiver of notice need not specify the purposes of the meeting unless such purposes were required to be specified in the notice of such meeting.

4.11 *Quorum.* At any meeting of the directors a majority of the directors then in office shall constitute a quorum. Any meeting may be adjourned by a majority of the votes cast upon the question, whether or not a quorum is present, and the meeting may be held as adjourned without further notice.

4.12 *Action by Vote.* When a quorum is present at any meeting, a majority of the directors present and voting shall decide any question, including election of officers, unless otherwise provided by law, the articles of organization, or these bylaws.

4.13 *Proxies.* Members may vote either in person or by written proxy dated not more than six months before the meeting named therein, which proxies shall be filed before being voted with the clerk or other person responsible for recording the proceedings of the meeting. Unless otherwise specifically limited by their terms, such proxies shall entitle the holders thereof to vote at any adjournment of the meeting but the proxy shall terminate after the final adjournment of such meeting.

4.14 *Action by Writing.* Any action required or permitted to be taken at any meeting of the directors may be taken without a meeting if all the directors consent to the action in writing and the written consents are filed with the records of the meetings of the directors. Such consents shall be treated for all purposes as a vote of a meeting.

4.15 *Compensation.* Directors shall be precluded from receiving compensation for their services but shall be entitled to receive such amount, if any, as the Directors may from time to time determine, to cover expenses of attendance at meetings.

Section 5. OFFICERS AND AGENTS

5.1 *Number and Qualification.* The officers of the corporation shall be a president, treasurer, clerk and such other officers, if any, as the directors may determine. The corporation may also have such agents, if any, as the directors may appoint. An officer may but need not be a director. The clerk shall be a resident of Massachusetts unless the corporation has a resident agent duly appointed for the purpose of service of process. A person may hold more than one office at the same time. If required by the directors, any officer shall give the corporation a bond for the faithful performance of his duties in such amount and with such surety or sureties as shall be satisfactory to the directors.

5.2 *Election.* The president, treasurer and clerk shall be elected annually by the directors at their first meeting. Other officers, if any, may be elected by the directors at any time.

5.3 *Tenure.* The president, treasurer and clerk shall be elected at the annual meeting and shall hold office until their successors are chosen.

5.4 *President.* The president shall be the chief executive officer of the corporation and, subject to the control of the directors, shall have general charge and supervision of the affairs of the corporation. The president shall preside at all meetings of the directors, except as the directors otherwise determine.

5.5 *Treasurer.* The treasurer shall be the chief financial officer and the chief accounting officer of the corporation. He shall be in charge of its financial affairs, funds, securities and valuable papers and shall keep full and accurate records thereof. He shall have such other duties and powers as designated by the directors or the president. He shall also be in charge of its books of account and accounting records, and of its accounting procedures.

5.6 *Clerk.* The clerk shall record and maintain records of all proceedings of the directors in a book or series of books kept for that purpose, which book or books shall be kept within the Commonwealth at the principal office of the corporation or at the office of its clerk or of its resident agent and shall be open at all reasonable times to the inspection of any person. Such book or books shall also contain records of all meetings of the incorporator and the original, or attested copies, of the articles of organization and bylaws and names of all directors and the address of each. If the clerk is absent from any meeting of members or directors, a temporary clerk chosen at the meeting shall exercise the duties of the clerk at the meeting.

5.7 *Suspension or Removal.* An officer may be suspended or removed with or without cause by vote of majority of directors then in office at any special meeting called for such purpose or at any regular meeting. An officer may be removed with cause only after reasonable notice and opportunity to be heard.

5.8 *Resignation.* An officer may resign by delivering his written resignation to the president, treasurer or clerk of the corporation, to a meeting of the directors, or to the corporation at its principal office. Such resignation shall be effective upon receipt (unless specified to be effective at some other time), and acceptance thereof shall not be necessary to make it effective unless it so states.

5.9 *Vacancies.* If the office of any officer becomes vacant, the directors may elect a successor. Each such successor shall hold office for the unexpired term, and in the case of the president, treasurer and clerk until his successor is elected and qualified, or in each case until he sooner dies, resigns, is removed or becomes disqualified.

Section 6. EXECUTION OF PAPERS

Except as the directors may generally or in particular cases authorize the execution thereof in some other manner, all deeds, leases, transfers, contracts, bonds, notes, checks, drafts and other obligations made, accepted or endorsed by the corporation shall be signed by the president or by the treasurer.

Any recordable instrument purporting to affect an interest in real estate, executed in the name of the corporation by two of its officers, of whom one is the president and the other is the treasurer, shall be binding on the corporation in favor of a purchaser or other person relying in good faith on such instrument notwithstanding any inconsistent provisions of the articles of organization, bylaws, resolutions or votes of the corporation.

Section 7. PERSONAL LIABILITY

The directors and officers of the corporation shall not be personally liable for any debt, liability or obligation of the corporation. All persons, corporations or other entities extending credit to, contracting with, or having any claim against, the corporation, may look only to the funds and property of the corporation for the payment of any such contract or claim, or for the payment of any debt, damages, judgment or decree, or of any money that may otherwise become due or payable to them from the corporation.

Section 8. AMENDMENTS

These bylaws may be altered, amended or repealed in whole or in part by vote of a majority of the directors then in office.

Section 9. PROCEDURE

Robert's Rules of Order shall govern the meetings of the board of Directors in all matters not provided for in these bylaws.

Appendix B — Sample Contracts

Master Contract Sample

(Name and address of booking agent goes here with phone number.)

AGREEMENT, as follows, made this .... day of ...., 19...... by and between .... herein called 'Artist,' contracting through .... herein called 'Artist's Manager' and .... herein called 'Local Manager' whose address is ....

1. Artist will perform the following services:

service #1: ...., place ....

in the city of ...., on ....19........

at .... o'clock in the ....

(remaining services detailed on rider A).

2. Local Manager agrees to furnish at its own expense a suitable theatre, hall or auditorium in said city, on the date and at the time for the performance(s) above mentioned, well heated, lighted, clean, and in good order, with a clean, comfortable dressing room near the stage for Artist, and to pay for taking show in and out and working same (if consisting of a company or troupe), furnishing all electricians and stage hands required, also to pay for all lights, tickets, house programs, license (if required), heating, cleaning, services of all necessary attaches, special police, ushers, ticket sellers for advance, or single sales (whether such sales take place in the theatre or elsewhere), ticket-takers, bill-posting, mailing and distributing of circulars and daily display news-paper advertising in the principal newspapers, and all other necessary expenses in connection therewith. NO SEATS WILL BE PERMITTED ON THE STAGE WITHOUT THE CONSENT OF ARTIST.

3. Local Manager represents that it has a lease for the theatre, hall or auditorium, covering the date or dates of this engagement, which lease will be shown to Artist or Artist's Manager upon request.

4. Local Manager agrees to furnish, without charge, properly tuned, one grand piano . . . for use at the above concert . . . unless Artist is able to and does obtain pianos without expense, through af-filiations with piano makers or dealers, and so advises Local Manager.

5. Artist agrees to supply the usual quantity of printing and ad-vertising material as available, and will also furnish copy of the program which is to be printed and distributed by the Local Manager. Local Manager hereby agrees to print said copy in its entirety.

6. In the event that Local Manager refuses or neglects to provide any of the items hereinbefore stated, Artist shall have the right to refuse

to perform this contract, and the Local Manager shall be liable to Artist for any damages on account thereof.

7. Not later than the first intermission of the first performance, or immediately before the performance if there is to be no intermission, Local Manager will deliver to ....

the sum of .... in lawful United States funds,

or by check payable to the order of ....
In the event that payments are not made as herein provided, Artist shall, at his or her option, have the right to refuse to continue the performance and Local Manager shall remain liable to Artist for the agreed price herein set forth, unless other arrangements for payment are explicitly set forth in riders to this contract.

8. If before the date of any scheduled concert, Artist or Artist's Manager finds that Local Manager has failed, neglected or refused to perform any contract with another artist for an earlier concert engagement, or if Artist or Artist's Manager finds that the financial credit of Local Manager has been impaired, Artist shall have the right to cancel this contract.

9. The Artist shall be under no liability for failure to appear or perform in the event that such failure is caused by or due to the physical disability of Artist, or acts or regulations of public authorities, labor difficulties, civil tumult, strike, epidemic, interruption or delay of transportation service, or any other cause beyond the control of Artist.

10. This contract cannot be assigned or transferred without the written consent of Artist's Manager, and contains the complete understanding of the parties respecting the subject matter hereof. It is not binding upon Artist until executed and delivered by the office of Artist's Manager and Artist's Manager signs only as Artist's agent and is not obligated hereunder and is not responsible for any acts or defaults of Artist.

11. No radio apparatus or transmitting device shall be used during the concert or concerts in any manner or form, in the building in which the concert or concerts shall be given, without the written consent of Artist or Artist's Manager.

12. This contract includes .... rider(s). The contract is not binding until all riders have been initialled by Local Manager and Artist or Artist's Manager.

ARTIST ....
BY ....

LOCAL MANAGER ....
BY ....

Failure to supply the following information may seriously interfere with the proper fulfillment of the contract by the Artist:

ATTRACTION ....

DATE ....

CITY ....

NAME OF HALL ....

HOUR OF CONCERT ....

HOUR OF REHEARSAL ....

BEST HOTEL (if hospitality not provided) ....
....

NAME AND ADDRESS OF PERSON MAKING CONTRACT

....

....

PARTY TO BE NOTIFIED ON ARRIVAL, ADDRESS AND TELE-PHONE NUMBER ....

....

....

SPECIAL INFORMATION

....

....

....

....

....

....

....

....

Rider A

service #............................., place ....

in the city of ...., on .... 19 ....

at .... o'clock in the ....

service #............................., place ....

in the city of ...., on .... 19........

at .... o'clock in the ....

Rider B

The company will carry its own technical staff. The company will request, in advance, additional workers (stagehands, loaders and unloaders) in the numbers required for the set-up, performance and strike of the show. In the past this has usually amounted to an additional _____ men. Local auspices is responsible for paying these workers.

If the number of additional stagehands as specified to the business agent of the local stagehands' union or directly to the auspices is not going to be present at the time of unloading, working the show and loading, the crew of the company will engage additional personnel; and the auspices will be responsible for paying these additional people at $35.00 per person, up to the number specified.

It is further agreed that the local auspices will be responsible for any additional local instrumentalists or any extra additional local stagehands that are demanded by the local union, including loaders in and loaders out.

Sponsor will provide the following basic equipment:
Front Lighting
A balcony rail (or cove) with no less than ten 750 watt Lekos (ellipsoidal instruments) on at least two circuits

Stage lighting
On first pipe electric (with no less than six circuits) seven 750 watt (500 watt is also acceptable) six by nine Lekos. And at least ten six-inch 500 watt Fresnels. Plus all necessary cable terminating in a 23 plate dimmer board.

Chairs and music stands
.... chairs; .... music stands; and .... stand lights.

Local manager shall be responsible for insuring compliance with all local and governmental rules in regard to the presentation.

Sample Musicians Contract

THIS CONTRACT for the personal services of the musicians on the engagement described below, made this .... day of .... 19....., between the undersigned Employer and .... musicians (including leader).

The musicians are engaged severally on the terms and conditions on the face hereof. The leader represents that the musicians already designated have agreed to be bound by said terms and conditions. Each musician yet to be chosen, upon acceptance shall be bound by said terms and conditions. The musicians severally agree to render services under the undersigned leader.

1. Name and Address of Place of Engagement ....
....
Name of Band or Group ....
2. Date(s), starting and finishing time of engagement(s), format ....
....
....
3. Type of Engagement (concert, workshop, residency) ....

4. Wage agreed upon (amount and terms) ....

....

Other considerations (transportation, meals, etc.) ....

....

ADDITIONAL TERMS AND CONDITIONS

If any musicians have not been chosen upon the signing of this contract, the Leader is responsible for the hiring of such persons and any replacements as are required.

In the event that the musicians fail to fulfill terms of this contract, the agreement is voided, but may be renegotiated at the Employer's discretion.

The agreement of the musicians to perform is subject to proven detention by sickness, accidents, riots, strikes, acts of God, or any other legitimate conditions beyond their control; such detention shall not jeopardize this contract.

No performance on the engagement shall be recorded, reproduced or transmitted from the place of performance by any means whatsoever, in the absence of a specific written agreement with the Leader relating to and permitting such recording, reproduction or transmission.

No musician will be required to perform any provisions of this contract or to render any services for the Employer as long as any prior claim is unsatisfied or unpaid, in whole or in part. If terms of this contract are not met by the employer, he shall pay the musicians in full as specified above.

....

....
Print Employer's Name   Print Leader's Name

X..   X..
Signature of Employer   Signature of Leader

....
Print Street Address   Print Street Address

....
City   State   Zip Code   City   State   Zip Code

....
Telephone   Telephone

                                                    ....
                                                    Booking Agent

Sample Theatre Contract

AGREEMENT, made this .... day of ...., 19........,
.... (hereinafter called "Company") and
.... (hereinafter called "Presentor").

    1. ENGAGEMENT Company agrees to provide a performing company of .... (hereinafter called the "play"), for .... performance(s), to take place on ...., at .... in the city of ....

    2. PAYMENT Presentor agrees to pay Company and Company agrees to accept as payment the sum of .... divided into three parts, the first third to be paid on signing of the contract, the second third to be paid at the end of the first performance and the third third to be paid at the end of the last performance.

    3. FACILITIES At the time and place specified above, the Presentor shall furnish a well-heated, lighted and licensed place for the performance(s) without charge to the Company.

    The Presentor agrees to supply the following at its own expense:

    a. The theater or hall for rehearsals one day prior to all first performances.

    b. Liability insurance to cover the performance or rehearsals at the theater or hall.

    c. Stagehands necessary for unloading, set-up, striking and reloading of Company's effects.

    d. Electricians and lighting operators requested by the Company for performances, rehearsals and set-up.

    e. All technical requirements as might be attached.

    f. Programs sufficient for the audience and accurately reproduced from copy supplied by Company.

    g. Presentor agrees to have playing area available for rehearsals at all times during engagement and there will be no striking of the show until the end of the last performance.

    4. PROMOTION AND PUBLICITY The Presentor shall advertise, display and announce the play in accordance with the instructions and information given by the Company.

    5. IMPOSSIBILITY OF PERFORMANCE In the event that the performance of the covenants of the Agreement on the part of the Company or Presentor shall be prevented by Act of God, physical disability, the acts or regulations of public authorities or labor unions, labor difficulties, strikes, civil tumult, campus disruption, war, epidemic, interruption or delay of transportation service or any cause beyond Company's or Presentor's reasonable control, Company and Presentor shall be respectively relieved of their obligations hereunder with respect to performance so prevented and Company shall be under no obligation to

present performance at any other time.

6. RESTRICTIONS Presentor agrees that no performance is to be recorded, broadcasted, televised, filmed or extended beyond the theater without the prior express written permission of the Company.

IN WITNESS WHEREOF the parties hereto have executed this agreement the day year first above written.

COMPANY: PRESENTOR:

....
By: ....
Witness: ....   Witness: ....
Address: ....   Address: ....
of Company ....   of Presentor ....
....
....

Appendix C — Sample Press Release

From: Molto Music Series   FOR IMMEDIATE RELEASE:
       Centerville, Massachusetts 01001   October 15, 1980
Contact: John Smith, Publicity Director
          617-777-0101

ROMA CHAMBER PLAYERS RETURN TO CENTERVILLE

They are coming back by popular demand! The Roma Chamber Players, after a triumphant tour of North America, will return to Centerville next Saturday, October 30. Their concert will begin at 8:15 P.M. and will be held in the Centerville Opera House. Tickets will be available at the Centerville Book Store or at the door.

Joanne Baker, President of the Molto Music Series, explains why her organization has invited these performers back: "We have received more favorable comments about their performance last year than on practically any event in our history. We feel fortunate that the Roma Chamber Players could fit us into their busy schedule again this year."

Since last year, the Roma Chamber Players have been heard in major cities across North America including New York, Boston, Toronto, and Los Angeles. Critical acclaim has followed the musicians wherever they have played. Said Michael Rineberg of the *Boston News:* "Over and above the fact that they are technically proficient, the group's musicianship is impeccable. It is a pleasure simply to sit back and listen."

George Smith, artistic director of the Roma Chamber Players, has promised an "exciting" evening of music. Smith claims that one of the works to be performed is particularly appropriate for the upcoming Halloween weekend. "We are planning to perform Beethoven's *Ghost* trio," he said, "and we hope it will serve as an appropriately electrifying welcome to Halloween." Susan Cook, a violinist in the group, explained that there were other reasons for the selection of the *Ghost* trio. "George is being modest," she said. "When we played Beethoven's *Archduke* trio last year, the Centerville audience gave us a standing ovation. The concert committee has asked us to program another Beethoven trio for this concert and the *Ghost* is one of our favorites."

Tickets for the concert are available at the Centerville Book Store and are priced at $2.50 and $4.00. If any tickets remain at concert time, they will be sold at the door. John Jones, head of the ticket committee, explained that the low ticket prices are possible because the concerts are partially underwritten by the National Endowment for the Arts and the State Council on the Arts and Humanities. In addition, a special grant from the Beller Foundation has made it possible to offer tickets to students and senior citizens at $1.50.

Appendix D —
Sample Fund-Raising Letter

Dear Friends:

With Molto Music's eleventh season successfully completed, it is time to take stock and to prepare for our annual metamorphosis. Next year, our program will be substantially different once again. As usual, there will be new faces on stage, new music, and new productions. Just as in each of the previous seasons, the coming one promises new growth and maturity.

As we look back, we can be proud of this season's accomplishments. The new auditorium, to which we moved with some apprehension, was filled with standing-room-only audiences for most events. Our budget increased by over 15%, thanks partly to a generous grant from the Beller Foundation and also to continuing support from our loyal contributors. Our school program continued to delight children of all ages. During the past year, 421 kids danced, sang, and clowned with fifteen professional performers.

And what is promised for next season? We will present our first mime show, with a week of mime workshops in the schools; we will initiate a reduced-price ticket program for senior citizens; and we will make substantial improvements in the auditorium's lighting system. Our plans promise growth not only in size but in quality.

It is crucial to our organization's continuing vitality that we continue to develop as we have in the past. It is the help of our friends that has made such growth possible. That help is made up of interest, enthusiasm, patience, moral support — and money. We are aware of the abundance of intangibles you have given us, and we shall always welcome them. Can you also celebrate the end of another wonderful season by sending a tax-deductible contribution that will help next year off to a flying start?

Sincerely,

Hubert Case   Judith Grey
Artistic Director   President of the Board

Appendix E — Procedure for Applying to the National Endowment for the Arts

I. Review the *Guide to Programs* (available from NEA, Washington, D.C., 20506).

II. Write and request printed guidelines for the specific program(s) in which you are interested.

III. When you receive the guidelines, review them VERY carefully. Does your organization meet preliminary eleigibility requirements? Are the programmatic elements and priorities for support expressed in the guidelines consistent with your organization's goals? Can you match the federal dollar *at least* one for one?

IV. BEFORE FILLING OUT AND SUBMITTING AN OFFICIAL APPLICATION:

A. Invest a few dollars and *call* the Program Information Office at the Endowment (202-634-6369). Ask for the telephone number of the particular program under whose guidelines you wish to apply.

B. *Call* that program office and ask for the "Program Specialist" in charge of applications submitted under your specific category in the guidelines. Introduce yourself to the Program Specialist, indicate that you have read the guidelines and are interested in applying, and that you would like him/her to call you back on the Government WATS (FTS) telephone line to discuss the project and application procedures.

C. Generally, the Program Specialist will call you back right away or within the day. When he/she calls, describe your project and its relevance to the guidelines. You will probably be asked questions on organizational structure, project budget, matching funds, and personnel. The Program Specialist may advise you immediately if the project is acceptable under program guidelines and, if so, will suggest that you submit a formal application. You should not take this to mean that the project will be funded.

Rather than give you an answer on the telephone, some Program Specialists will ask that you send a written draft proposal of your project *before* submitting an actual application. This draft proposal should have the following three elements:

1. *Project Description:* Be sure this description (no more than one page) clearly defines the entire scope of the project and the estimated impact with a minimum of philosophical rhetoric.

2. *Budget:* Expenses and Income should be line-itemed, with no undefined entries like ''miscellaneous'' or ''contingency'' expenses. Remember that the Endowment will fund no more than 50% of the project cost — and usually less. Do not request *more* than 50%. Be sure that all figures add properly and that the budget balances — that the total cost of the project (total expenditure) equals income plus the amount requested from NEA.

3. *Personnel:* Include a one-paragraph resume on each person charged with directorial or administrative responsibility for the project. Include brief resumes on all artistic personnel to be used on the project.

Program Specialists are your most valuable contact at the Endowment. They are trained to answer your questions on almost every topic, or to know where to find the answers. They are ''on your side,'' so be pleasant and personal in your approach to them. Not only are they generally experts in their own right, with substantial artistic or administrative credentials, but they have to respond daily to a national constituency and are overworked. Do not be frivolous or demanding with their time.

D. If you are told that the project is not appropriate to the guidelines, ask if there are other programs at the Endowment under which you might apply. If your are referred to another program, repeat all the steps under ''IV'' above.

V. Call your NEA Regional Representative (your state arts agency can provide you with this person's name, address, and phone number). Arrange for a site visit and discuss your application in detail. Also call your state arts agency and alert the staff that you will be submitting an application to the Endowment. Ask for help and advice.

VI. Before you fill out the application, *carefully read* the application form instructions. If there is something you do not understand, call the Program Specialist. If your description of the project does not fit into the space provided, it is too long! Include all required supplementary materials specified in the guidelines. Type the application — do not submit a handwritten one. Do not forget to sign and date it. The application should be postmarked no later than the application deadline date. If there is a problem submitting before the deadline, call the Program Specialist and ask if an extension is possible.

VII. Applications are reviewed first by a panel of advisors who make recommendations to the National Council on the Arts. The Council reviews the panel recommendations and makes its own recommendations to the Chairman of NEA, in whom final authority for the decision rests. This whole process takes slightly less than a year; and, generally, it is not advisable to try to find out what the recommendation of the panel or Council has been on your application. Specific questions about the procedure and the timing can be answered by Program Specialists, but do not badger them for information which they cannot provide.

VIII. Generally speaking, no news is good news. Rejections are sent out immediately at various stages of the review process. Grant award letters are often delayed several months past the final decision date.

Appendix F — Technical Glossary*

General Stage Terminology

On The Stage

Directions. In the theatre, directions are *always* given in terms of *stage left* and *stage right*. This is the *Performer's* left hand and right hand as he faces the audience. *Upstage* and *downstage* are terms that originated in the time of raked stages when the back of the stage floor was slanted higher than the front. Thus the portion of the stage closest to the audience is downstage and the back of the stage is upstage.

Proscenium Arch. The opening in the downstage wall separating the audience and the stage.

Fly Loft. The space directly above the stage where draperies and lighting instruments are hung. Ideally, the height of the fly loft is three times as high as the proscenium arch.

Grid. The metal framework at the top of the fly loft just below the stage roof. Everything that flies is suspended from the grid.

Work lights. Lights that fully illuminate stage and wings, used primarily during rehearsals and mid-performance set changes.

Fly System. A series of cables, pulleys (called sheaves and pronounced shivs), and counter weights that enable scenery, drapes, or lighting equipment to fly in and out. There are two basic types of fly systems. The *hemp system* uses hemp ropes to support the battens, and the counterbalance is a large sand bag. This is a very old system but works well in the hands of a competent fly man. The more modern system is the *counterweight system*. The battens are supported by metal aircraft cable, and the counterbalances are steel or iron counterweights held in a large metal arbor.

Line Set. A group of three to five lines used together to lift a batten.

Batten. A metal pipe attached to the cables of the fly system on which all scenery and lighting equipment is tied or clamped.

Trim. A mark designating the height of a batten when it is in a working position.

Plaster Line. A line drawn across the stage at the upstage edge of the proscenium. It is at this point that all measurements up and down stage are made. This is one of the two major points of reference used in

*This glossary has been reprinted by permission of Western States Arts Foundation from its *Technical Production Handbook* by M.K. Barrell. Copies of the *Technical Production Handbook* may be ordered from Western States Arts Foundation, 428 East 11th Street, Denver, Colorado 80203.

measuring a stage.

Curtain Line. The line on the stage where the act curtain (see masking) falls. Used as a measurement point for up and down stage much like the plaster line. It is not as accurate a measurement as the plaster line, since the curtain can shift and the curtain's fullness is often forgotten in measuring.

Center Line. The other major point for measurement on the stage. It is a line running directly down the middle of the stage separating stage left from stage right. All measurements on the stage are made from the plaster line and the center line.

Ground Plan. An aerial view of the stage drawn to a specific scale (usually one-quarter inch equals one foot or one-half inch equals one foot) showing all the pertinent elements of the stage.

Light Plot. A ground plan of the stage with all the lighting instruments drafted on, showing where each lighting instrument is hung, what type it is, what dimmer it is patched into, what circuit it is plugged into, and what color it is gelled.

Masking

Masking. Any drapery or scenic piece used to define the stage or hide the view of the audience.

Border or Teaser. A horizontal masking piece used to hide anything in the fly loft such as lighting equipment and scenery.

Leg. A vertical masking piece hung at the sides of the stage used to hide the wing spaces.

Wing. The offstage space between the legs.

Grand Drape. The first (downstage) border often called a teaser. It is the visual determiner of the height of the proscenium opening (called the trim height). It is not the main curtain that opens and closes.

Tormentor or Torm. The first (downstage) leg. It can be a soft drapery but is often framed and solid. This is the visual determiner of the width of the stage.

House Curtain or Act Curtain. This is the curtain that opens and closes separating the audience from the stage. It is usually hung directly upstage of the grand drape.

Asbestos. A fire-resistant curtain located at the proscenium opening.

Cyclorama. A very large fabric drop rigged at the back of the stage and wrapping downstage in the wing space. Its primary use is to give a feeling of great depth. Usually not very applicable for dance as the downstage curved portion provides a barrier that makes exits and sidelighting very difficult.

Sky Drop. A fabric drop at the back of the stage used for sky effects without wrapping downstage like a cyclorama.

Scrim. A transparent gauze material used for ghosts, clouds, and any effect requiring something to appear and disappear. When lit from the front, it becomes opaque; when back lit, it becomes transparent. Often used in front of a skydrop to give more sense of depth.

Instrument Mounting Positions

Electric. A batten with cable and connectors mounted on it specifically used for hanging instruments.

Bridge. The term for the first downstage electric when there is a large trusswork instead of the simple batten. The bridge was originally designed so a stage hand could move about to adjust the carbons of early carbon-arc spotlights.

Boom. A vertical pipe used for mounting instruments. On stage booms are usually portable. When mounted in the audience, they are usually a permanent fixture. The terms tree, tower and ladder are often used for a portable boom.

House Boom. A permanent boom mounted in the house.

Box Boom. A boom mounted in a box seat.

Balcony Boom. A boom mounted in the balcony.

Balcony Rail. A mounting position on the front edge of the balcony. Very popular for musical comedy but rarely used for dance lighting.

Beam Slot. A false beam mounted in the ceiling of the auditorium used for a mounting position. Beam slot has become the term for any horizontal ceiling mounting position.

F.O.H. Front of House. Any mounting position in the auditorium.

A.P. Ante-Pro. Any mounting position in the auditorium.

Lighting Equipment
Instruments

The general name for any light that is specifically designed to be used on the stage is *instrument*. You can call any stage light an instrument and you're calling it correctly, like calling a Ford a car. You shouldn't call it a light (that's what it emits), and you shouldn't call it a lamp (a lamp is the glass bulb inside the instrument that creates the light).

There are two general groups of instruments, *spotlights* and *floodlights*. These terms are very rarely used without specific qualification.

Spotlights are by far the most common group of theatre instruments. There are two major types of spotlights: *Lekos* and *Fresnels*. Between them, these two types account for ninety-five percent of all normally used instruments.

Fresnel (pronounced fre-nel) are correctly Fresnel-lens spotlights. Fresnel is this instrument's only correct name, but terms such as juniors, coffee grinders, or inkies are common slang usually used to specify a certain size. Fresnels come in several sizes which are measured by the diameter of the lens. Six and eight inch lenses are the most common, although Fresnels are manufactured all the way from three inches to thirty inches. Fresnels give a wide beam, soft-edged light that does certain lighting jobs very well. An even, patternless wash of the stage from overhead is best handled by Fresnels as they blend with one another very well. The beam of light cannot be shaped well and this greatly limits the use of Fresnels from positions where precise beam control is needed. Common accessories for a Fresnel are *barn doors.* These are movable blades affixed to the front of a Fresnel that allow the beam of light to be shaped slightly and kept off the background or audience. There are dozens of companies manufacturing Fresnels and, since they are quite simple in their design, most are of good quality. Purchasing one of the cheaper brands will usually give you acceptable light.

Leko is an acronym of the names of the two men who developed the instrument. Although technically incorrect, the name Leko has become as commonly used for this instrument as the name Kleenex has for tissue paper. The correct name of a Leko is ellipsoidal-reflector spotlight. It is often called an ellipsoidal, or an ERS. Brand names compound the confusion because the rights to the term Leko were purchased nine years ago by the Lighting Corporation of America, later to become Strand-Century, Inc. Strand-Century's brand of ERS is, therefore, called a Lekolite. Not to be outdone, Kleigl Brothers (the other giant in the stage equipment industry) calls their ERS a Kleiglite. Add to this an untold number of slang terms and the situation becomes truly boggled. One reason there are so many names associated with Lekos is they are the workhorse of all instruments. They are the most powerful, the most efficient and the most flexible of all stage lighting instruments. The Leko has a hard-edged beam of light that can be easily shaped and controlled to allow the light to be focused where it's needed and cut off of any object that shouldn't be illuminated such as a leg or the proscenium arch. They can have patterns, called gobos, inserted into them that can shape the light to any outline, projecting any shape from trees to stars.

There are complexities, however, that make dealing with a Leko difficult. On a Fresnel the beam of light can be adjusted from a wide beam to a narrow spot. The Leko, on the other hand, has a fixed beam spread. The size of the beam remains the same even though the edges can be made hard or soft. To achieve a different beam spread it is necessary to change the lenses to a different focal-length lens system. There are two numbers used in designating any Leko, the first is the diameter of the lens (as with the Fresnel) and the second is the focal length used. The longer the focal length, the narrower the beam. Therefore, a 6 x 9 Lekolite would have a lens diameter of six inches and a focal length of nine inches, and would be considered a medium beam spread instrument. A 6 x 12 Lekolite would look exactly like a 6 x 9 on the outside but would have a narrow beam and a more intense light.

There are more complications with the additions of step-down barrels, stepped lenses, and single versus double lens systems. The complexities of the optics of a Leko can confuse the best technicians, yet the information is crucial. Knowing the diameter of a Leko is absolutely no good without knowing the lens type and focal length.

The quality of light emitted by a Leko varies greatly from manufacturer to manufacturer. The design relationship of the lens, lamp, and the reflector is so complex that only the very best Lekos give off a good quality light. Although there are exceptions, a cheap Leko is often no better than no Leko at all. Lekos are very expensive. They cannot be substituted for effectively, and dance designers use them extensively. Some designers use them exclusively.

Floodlights are the other major subgroup of instruments. The primary difference between spotlights and floodlights is the lens. All spotlights have a lens and all floodlights don't. The floodlights, therefore, do not allow the operator to change the shape or size of the beam of light. The very first type of incandescent stage lighting was a form of floodlight known as a border striplight. It was nothing but a long sheet metal trough filled with a row of small wattage, household type "A" lamps. It gave illumination to the stage much the way flourescent tubes illuminate a modern office space. There are still derivations of the original borderstrip in use today, usually called either a striplight or a borderlight (the term X-ray is an old expression designating the first row of borderlights.) Their only real purpose in lighting dance is in lighting backdrops and cycloramas, which they do very well. In theatre, however, they are used extensively for toning and blending.

Footlights. While footlights are rarely, if ever, used in dance because exposed footlights are hazardous to dancers, they are used in theatres. They are the best location for theatre toning and are also useful on low level for musicals, opaquing downstage scrims, and as curtain warmers.

A follow spot can simply be a modification of a Leko or it can be a very high-powered carbon-arc lamp. It has little use in modern dance or naturalistic theatre but is quite common in ballet and musical comedy. Follow spots are highly adjustable as to the size and softness of the beam, but the skill of the operator is crucial. A bad follow-spot operator can ruin any performance.

These are the primary instruments used in stage lighting. Every once in a while, a mutant will appear from one of the smaller manufacturers. Most are of little value. Homemade instruments from old coffee cans or World War II fighter plane nose cones are still lurking in many old closets. Instruments like these are acceptable for a classroom choreographic showing but are not valid for a legitimate concert.

Dimmers

The dimming system controls the light intensity of each instrument. There are two major groupings: manual and remotely controlled electronic types.

Manual dimmers are either resistance or auto-transformer types. They are both operated the same way although the auto-transformer is a more modern and efficient piece of equipment. Both are cumbersome, require several operators and cannot follow complex, sophisticated cues. When working on a manual board, a lighting designer who is used to working on an electronic dimmer will have to greatly simplify his cues and, therefore, his effectiveness. The main benefit of manual dimmer boards is that they are nearly indestructible, and many theatres that use entirely untrained operators swear by them because they are easy to operate.

Electronic dimmers are usually of the SCR (silicon-controlled rectifier) type, although there are some early models still in use of the thyrotron tube type. The main advantage of an electronic dimmer is it can be remotely controlled by a single operator. It has the ability to be pre-set by various means (cards, pre-set ranks, or computers) and allows an incredible degree of flexibility and sophistication in executing cues. Since electronic dimmers are fragile, they need regular maintenance. When telling the company technician about your dimming system, it is important to let them know how many dimmers are actually operating.

Patch Panels And Circuitry

The maze of cables that connect the instruments to the dimmers is known as the *circuitry*. These cables, either visible or concealed, go from the mounting positions on the stage to a large panel that often looks like a telephone switchboard. This is the *patch panel* or Quick-Connect. It enables the technician to plug any circuit, and, thus, any instrument into any dimmer. The patch panel is a very important feature of any good lighting system because it allows maximum use of each dimmer.

A very important thing to know about the circuitry when trying to integrate your equipment with someone else's is the configuration of the connectors, commonly called outlets. There are several different types of connectors and none of them are compatible with the others. It is necessary to make adaptors from one connector to another. Most companies that travel with some of their own equipment also travel with adaptors to other types of connectors.

About the American Council for the Arts

The American Council for the Arts (ACA) is the only national organization working on behalf of all the arts. For more than 20 years, ACA has provided leadership in innovative programs and services for artists and arts organizations all across the country.

ACA is a unique combination of management consulting firm, publishing house, information center, and advocate for all the arts. Among its major accomplishments are the following:

- Helping to create and continue the National Endowment for the Arts
- Publishing *American Arts* magazine as well as over 50 books on arts and arts management
- Producing landmark conferences on such subjects as "Business and the Arts" and "The Arts and Tourism"
- Developing a wide variety of programs for arts leaders

Major contributors to ACA at the time of publication:

Aetna Life & Casualty Company
   Foundation
Jane Alexander
Allied Chemical Foundation
The Allstate Foundation
American Express Foundation
American Telephone & Telegraph
   Company
Atlantic Richfield Company
Bankers Trust Company
Anne Bartley
Bechtel Foundation
Polly Bergen
Edward M. Block
Boise Cascade Corporation
Bozell & Jacobs, Inc.
The Bristol-Myers Fund
Carter Hawley Hale Stores, Inc.
CBS Inc.
Chase Manhattan Bank
Chevron USA, Inc.
The Coca-Cola Company
Marshall Cogan
Connecticut General Insurance
   Corporation
Conoco, Inc.
The Continental Group Foundation
Cummins Engine Foundation
Cunningham & Walsh, Inc.
Disney Foundation
Emerson Electric Company
Estee Lauder Companies
Ethyl Corporation
Exxon Corporation
Federated Department Stores, Inc.
Ford Motor Company Fund
Mrs. Robert Fowler
Arthur Gelber
General Felt Industries
Grace Foundation
Gulf & Western Foundation
Hanes Dye & Finishing Company
Louis Harris & Associates
Hercules, Incorporated
Heublein Foundation
IBM Corporation

International Telephone & Telegraph
   Company
John Kilpatrick, Jr.
Mrs. Fred Lazarus III
Mrs. Edward Marcus
Metropolitan Life Foundation
Mobil Foundation
Monsanto Fund
National Endowment for the Arts
National Westminster Bank, Ltd.
NL Industries Foundation
New York State Council on the Arts
J.C. Penney Company, Inc.
The Pfizer Foundation
Philip Morris Incorporated
Phillips Petroleum Foundation
Pogo Producing Company
The Procter & Gamble Company
Prudential Insurance Company
   Foundation
RCA Corporation
R.J. Reynolds Industries, Inc.
Sakowitz, Inc.
Scurlock Foundation
Sears, Roebuck & Company
Mr. & Mrs. Alfred Shands III
Shell Companies Foundation
TICOR
Times-Mirror Company
Tosco Corporation
Union Pacific Foundation
United California Bank Foundation
U.S. Gypsum Foundation
United States Steel Foundation
Mrs. Thomas Wachtell
Mr. & Mrs. Gerald H. Westby
Western Electric Fund
Westinghouse Electric Fund
Xerox Corporation